Windo
for Beginners

Books Available

By the same authors:

BP538   Windows XP for Beginners*
BP525   Controlling Windows XP the easy way*
BP522   Microsoft Works Suite 2002 explained
BP514   Windows XP explained*
BP513   IE 6 and Outlook Express 6 explained*
BP512   Microsoft Access 2002 explained
BP511   Microsoft Excel 2002 explained
BP510   Microsoft Word 2002 explained
BP509   Microsoft Office XP explained
BP498   Using Visual Basic
BP493   Windows Me explained*
BP491   Windows 2000 explained*
BP487   Quicken 2000 UK explained*
BP486   Using Linux the easy way*
BP465   Lotus SmartSuite Millennium explained
BP433   Your own Web site on the Internet
BP341   MS-DOS explained
BP284   Programming in QuickBASIC
BP258   Learning to Program in C

If you would like to purchase a Companion Disc for any of the listed books by the same authors, apart from the ones marked with an asterisk, containing the file/program listings which appear in them, then fill in the form at the back of the book and send it to Phil Oliver at the stipulated address.

Windows XP for Beginners

by

N. Kantaris

and

P.R.M. Oliver

Bernard Babani (publishing) Ltd
The Grampians
Shepherds Bush Road
London W6 7NF
England

www.babanibooks.com

Please Note

Although every care has been taken with the production of this book to ensure that any projects, designs, modifications and/or programs, etc., contained herewith, operate in a correct and safe manner and also that any components specified are normally available in Great Britain, the Publishers and Author(s) do not accept responsibility in any way for the failure (including fault in design) of any project, design, modification or program to work correctly or to cause damage to any equipment that it may be connected to or used in conjunction with, or in respect of any other damage or injury that may be so caused, nor do the Publishers accept responsibility in any way for the failure to obtain specified components.

Notice is also given that if equipment that is still under warranty is modified in any way or used or connected with home-built equipment then that warranty may be void.

© 2003 BERNARD BABANI (publishing) LTD

First Published - August 2003

British Library Cataloguing in Publication Data:

A catalogue record for this book is available from the British Library

ISBN 0 85934 538 6

Cover Design by Gregor Arthur.
Printed and Bound in Great Britain by Cox & Wyman Ltd., Reading.

About this Book

Windows XP for Beginners was written to help people who recently bought a computer with the Windows XP Professional or Home edition operating system (the latter being a cut-down version of the former). The most frequent question which comes to mind is "having bought the computer, what can I do with it now?"

Answers might include; keeping in touch with your children or grandchildren, browsing the Internet to get some useful information, downloading the photographs from your digital camera and storing them on the computer's hard disc, or simply getting to grips with simple word processing, or running educational programs for your offspring. The choice is endless.

Whatever your reasons for buying a computer, it is very important to understand its operating system (in this case Windows XP), because it is the operating system that allows you to run other programs, store and retrieve information, and looks after the health of your PC.

The material in this book is presented using a simple language, avoiding jargon as much as possible, but with such a subject some is inevitable, so a glossary of terms is included, which should be used with the text of this book where necessary. The book is structured on the 'what you need to know first, appears first' basis, although you don't have to start at the beginning and go right through to the end, as the chapters have been designed to be fairly self-contained.

The present book was written with the non technical, non computer literate person in mind. It is hoped that with its help you will be able to get the most out of your computer, when using Windows XP, and that you will be able to do it in the shortest, most effective and enjoyable way. Have fun!

If, however, you are upgrading your computer's operating system from a previous version of Windows to Windows XP and want to know what preparations you need to make to your system, as well as how to use all its tools and the accessory programs that come with it, then may we suggest you take a look at our book *Windows XP explained* (BP514), also published by Bernard Babani (publishing) Ltd.

About the Authors

Noel Kantaris graduated in Electrical Engineering at Bristol University and after spending three years in the Electronics Industry in London, took up a Tutorship in Physics at the University of Queensland. Research interests in Ionospheric Physics, led to the degrees of M.E. in Electronics and Ph.D. in Physics. On return to the UK, he took up a Post-Doctoral Research Fellowship in Radio Physics at the University of Leicester, and then in 1973 a lecturing position in Engineering at the Camborne School of Mines, Cornwall, (part of Exeter University), where between 1978 and 1997 he was also the CSM IT Manager. At present he is IT Director of FFC Ltd.

Phil Oliver graduated in Mining Engineering at Camborne School of Mines in 1967 and since then has specialised in most aspects of surface mining technology, with a particular emphasis on computer related techniques. He has worked in Guyana, Canada, several Middle Eastern and Asian countries, South Africa and the United Kingdom, on such diverse projects as: the planning and management of bauxite, iron, gold and coal mines; rock excavation contracting in the UK; international mining equipment sales and international mine consulting. In 1988 he took up a lecturing position at Camborne School of Mines (part of Exeter University) in Surface Mining and Management. He retired from this in 1998, to spend more time writing, consulting and developing Web sites for clients.

Acknowledgements

We would like to thank friends and colleagues, for their helpful tips and suggestions which assisted us in the writing of this book.

Trademarks

HP and LaserJet are registered trademarks of Hewlett Packard Corporation.

Microsoft, Windows, and Windows XP, are either registered trademarks or trademarks of Microsoft Corporation.

PostScript is a registered trademark of Adobe Systems Incorporated.

All other brand and product names used in the book are recognised as trademarks, or registered trademarks, of their respective companies.

Contents

1. **Package Overview**. 1
   The Windows XP Start Menu. 2
      User Accounts. 5
      Exercises. 7
   Right-click Menus. 9
   Parts of a Window. 10
   Activity Related Tasks. 15
   The Mouse Pointers. 16
   Using the Help System. 17
   Exiting Windows XP. 19

2. **The Windows Environment**. 21
   The Common Toolbar Buttons. 23
   The Menu Bar Options. 25
      Dialogue Boxes. 27
      Exercises. 30
   Taskbar Buttons. 32
   Manipulating Windows. 34
      Changing the Active Window. 34
      Sizing a Window. 35
      Moving Windows and Dialogue Boxes. 35
      Minimising and Maximising Windows. 36
      Closing a Window. 36
      Exercises. 37
   Windows Display Arrangement. 38
      Exercises. 39

3. **Working with Files and Folders** 41

   Creating a New Folder. 42

   Searching for Files and Folders. 44

      Filename Convention. 45

      Search Results. 46

   Selecting Files and Folders. 47

   Copying or Moving Files and Folders. 48

   Sending Files and Folders. 50

      Exercises. 52

   Creating Shortcuts. 53

   Deleting Files or Folders. 54

   The Recycle Bin. 55

      Exercises. 56

   Other Image Folder Views. 57

      Previewing an Image. 58

      The Filmstrip View. 59

   Copying Files or Folders to a CD. 60

   Compressing Files and Folders. 61

      Exercises. 64

4. **Controlling your PC** 65

   The Windows Control Panel. 65

   Changing your Display. 68

   Controlling Printers. 71

      Configuring your Printer. 73

      Managing Print Jobs. 74

   Installing a Fax Printer. 75

      The Fax Console. 79

   The Address Book. 80

      Address Book Help. 82

   Adding Hardware to your System. 83

Adding Software to your PC. 84
    Adding/Removing Windows Features. 85
Checking your Regional Settings. 86

5. E-mail - Outlook Express Basics. 89

Modem Properties. 89
Microsoft Outlook Express. 90
    Connecting to your Server. 91
Receiving an E-mail. 96
    Sending a Test E-mail Message. 97
The Main Outlook Express Window. 98
    The Folders List. 98
    The Contacts Pane. 99
    The Message List. 99
    The Preview Pane. 100
    Message Status Icons. 101
    The Main Window Toolbar. 102
The Read Message Window. 103
    The Read Message Toolbar. 104
    Signing your E-mail. 104
The New Message Window. 105
    Using Message Stationery. 106
    The New Message Toolbar. 106
    Message Formatting. 107
Replying to a Message. 109
Removing Deleted Messages. 109

6. E-mail - Some Other Features. 111

Using E-mail Attachments. 111
    Sending an E-mail to the Drafts Folder. 113
    Receiving Attachments with an E-mail. 114
    Organising your Messages. 115
    The System Folders. 116
Spell Checking your Messages. 118
Connection at Start-up. 120
Printing your Messages. 122
Using Message Rules. 123
    The Blocked Senders List. 126
The Address Book in Outlook Express. 127
Outlook Express Help. 130

7. Using the Internet Explorer. 131

Your PC Settings. 133
Searching the Web. 134
The Address Bar. 137
The Standard Toolbar. 138
Favorites. 140
    Adding a Favorite. 142
History Files. 143
    The Cache. 145
Msn Hotmail. 146
Explorer Help. 150

8. Accessibility, Scanners and Cameras. . . 153

    The Keyboard Options. 155
    The Sound Options. 155
    The Display Options. 156
    The Mouse Options. 157
    The General Options. 159

The Microsoft Magnifier. 161
The On-Screen Keyboard. 163
Using a Scanner or Camera. 166
E-mailing Scanner and Camera Pictures. 171
Sending Video Clips as Attachments. 172

9. Looking After your PC. 179

Problem Prevention. 179
System File Protection. 180
Automatic Update. 180
System Restore. 184
Activating the Firewall. 187
Disk Cleanup. 188
Scanning a Hard Disc for Errors. 189
Defragmenting your Hard Discs. 191
Scheduled Tasks. 192
Power Saving Management. 196
Hibernation Mode. 196
Standby Mode. 198
On Turning your Computer Off. 200
Backing up your Data. 201
Making a Back-up. 201
Retrieving Back-up Files. 207
Adding Files and Folders to a Back-up. 208

10. Glossary of Terms. 211

Index. 231

1

Package Overview

Windows XP (XP for eXPerience) is available in two flavours; the Home edition (less expensive) and the Professional edition (more expensive, but with additional features such as more options for networking computers with added security and simplified management). The latter edition also includes features for power users, such as enhanced file security, remote access to the computer's desktop and a personal Web server.

Although we have used Windows XP Professional to write this book, we will only cover what is common with the Windows XP Home edition, as most home PC users will find that these common options between the two editions contain all the facilities they will ever need.

In Windows XP, Microsoft has adopted the Tasks pane approach which allows easy manipulation of files and folders which helps with the management of your data, such as word processed documents, photographs, etc. Tasks panes also provide you with an easy way for carrying out a host of other operations, such as printing, scanning, faxing, downloading or publishing information on the Web. In Windows XP the content of a Tasks pane changes to accommodate what you are doing at the time. In what follows, we assume that Windows XP has been installed on your computer and is up and running.

The Windows XP Start Menu

Switching on your PC automatically loads Windows XP. Below (Fig. 1.1) we show the Windows XP working screen, called the 'Desktop', with one item on the bottom right of it identified as the **Recycle Bin**. In addition, the ***start*** button at the bottom left corner of the Windows screen has been clicked with the left mouse button to display the two-column ***start*** menu.

The left menu column provides shortcuts to the **Internet Explorer**, **Outlook Express**, and the six applications used most often (in your case these will most likely be totally different as they can be changed). On the right column there are shortcuts to **My Documents**, **My Computer**, **Control Panel**, etc., which are normally common to all users.

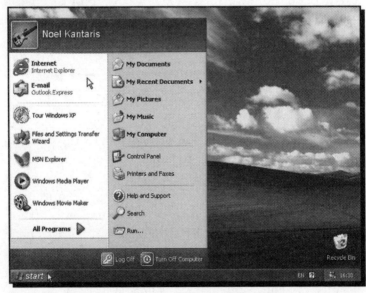

Fig. 1.1 The Windows XP Start Menu Screen.

If your computer is already capable of being connected to the Internet (if not don't worry as we will show you how to do this in detail later on), you could then use the Internet Explorer program that comes bundled with the operating system to surf the Net, or the Outlook Express program to send and receive e-mail. These two programs will be discussed in some detail later on.

Windows XP also comes with a number of features, such as 'Communications' and 'Entertainment' utilities, 'System Tools', the 'Paint' graphics program, the 'Picture and Fax Viewer', and the adequate word processor 'WordPad'. Some of these will be discussed in some detail in the following chapters of this book as they form the core of the tools you need to master so as to keep your computer healthy and your data safe. Of course, Windows XP (particularly the Professional edition) caters for many new technological developments, but we shall not be delving into these as they are beyond the scope of this book.

Finally, Windows XP can manage all other programs that run on your computer, such as fully featured word processors, spreadsheets, databases, games, and many more. For example, hovering with the mouse pointer over

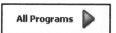

the **All Programs** button, shown here (also see the bottom of Fig. 1.1 for its position on the screen), displays the first column of the cascade menu where all Windows applications are to be found. In Fig. 1.2 on the next page we show some of the contents of the **All Programs** available on one of our computers, as well as the contents of the Windows Accessories mentioned above.

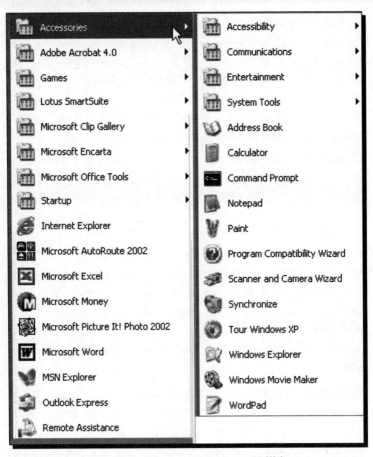

Fig. 1.2 The Windows Accessory Utilities.

Note that entries in menu lists such as the **Accessories** that have an arrow head (▸) to the right of their name as in the case of **Accessibility**, **Communications**, **Entertainment** and **System Tools**, contain additional lists of utilities, while entries such as the **Address Book**, **Windows Movie Maker** and **WordPad**, to mention but a few, are self-contained programs.

User Accounts

At the top of the *start* menu the name of the current user is displayed with a picture against it. Left-clicking this picture opens the User Accounts screen shown in Fig. 1.3. From here you can choose a different picture for the current user either from the ones supplied or from one of your own. You can also change the Computer's theme, desktop, screen savers, etc. - more about these later.

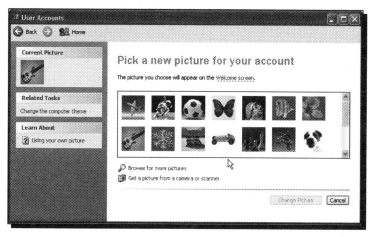

Fig. 1.3 The User Accounts Dialogue Box.

As we mentioned earlier, Windows XP has the ability to adapt the first of its two-column menus to the way you use your computer. It keeps track of what features and programs you use the most and adds them to the list at the bottom of the left column. For example, if you use **WordPad** by selecting it from the Accessories sub-menu, next time you click the *start* button you will see this application pinned to the bottom of the first column of the *start* menu. This saves time as you don't have to scroll through menu lists to find the application you want to use.

To remove an application from the first column of the *start* menu, right-click it with your mouse and select **Remove from This List**, as shown in Fig. 1.4. This removes the name of the application from the list, not the application itself from your hard disc.

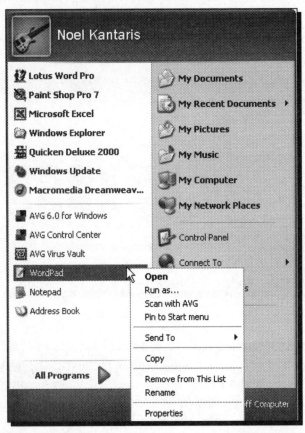

Fig. 1.4 Simultaneous Display of Running Applications.

You also have a menu option to **Pin to Start menu** any selected program. This adds it to the top of the left column of the *start* menu which is a more permanent list.

You can also use this facility to pin your favourite programs, even if these are to be found in the **All Programs** menu or its sub-menus, to the top of the left column of the *start* menu, thus customising the way you run your computer.

Exercises

If you have read so far, do try the following exercises:

I. To change the picture that represents you as a user:

- Left-click the *start* button to display its menu.

- Place the mouse pointer on the picture at the top left of the *start* menu (your picture could be different than the one shown here), and when it changes to a pointing hand, as shown to the right, left-click it to open the User Accounts dialogue box shown in Fig. 1.3.

- Select a different picture to represent you by left-clicking one from the displayed list and left-click the **Change Picture** button at the bottom of the dialogue box.

II. To pin your favourite programs on the top left column of the *start* menu:

- Left-click the *start* button to display the *start* menu.

- Hover with the mouse pointer over the **All Programs** button to display the *start* menu.

- Move the mouse pointer on your chosen program to highlight it and right-click it to display its shortcut menu (see next section), then left-click the **Pin to Start menu** option to pin the selected program to the top of the left column of the *start* menu.

Once you have pinned your chosen programs to the *start* menu, you could rename them, if you so wished, using the right-click menu, or you could move their position on the list to suit your preferences.

To move an item on the *start* menu, point to it to highlight it, then press the left mouse button and while keeping it pressed, drag the mouse pointer to the desired position on the list. Letting go of the mouse button, fixes the item in selected position. Fig. 1.5 shows Microsoft Word being moved to just below Microsoft Excel.

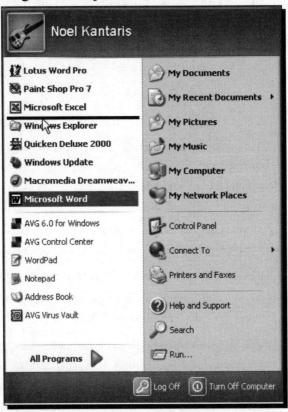

Fig. 1.5 Moving an Application on the **Start** Menu List.

Right-click Menus

To see another right-click menu (also known as a shortcut menu) containing the most common commands applicable to, say, the desktop, point with your mouse to an empty part of it and right-click. This displays the menu shown in Fig. 1.6. From this menu you can select how to **Arrange Icons** on your desktop, **Paste** a shortcut icon on it, or create a **New** folder for your favourite program.

Fig. 1.6 The Desktop Right-click Menu.

Right-clicking the **Recycle Bin** icon on the desktop, reveals the options in Fig. 1.7.

Fig. 1.7 The Recycle Bin Right-click Menu.

In this case we have the option to **Open** the Recycle Bin which has the same effect as double-clicking its icon with the left mouse button, **Explore** its contents, **Empty** it of its contents, or display its **Properties**.

If you were to right-click a program icon on the **All Programs** menu, such as that of a word processor, if one was installed on your computer, you would find that different options to those of the Recycle Bin are being offered. For example, the option to delete or rename such a program is included (we do not recommend you do so), while the **Recycle Bin** icon does not offer such options.

Parts of a Window

Do spend some time looking at the various parts that make up the Windows screen - we use the word 'Windows' to refer to the whole environment, while the word 'windows' refers to application or document windows. Below we show **My Computer** which is opened by clicking on the *start* button and then clicking its entry on the top-right column of the displayed menu. To see what appears below, left-click the **View** menu command and select **Icons** from the displayed sub-menu.

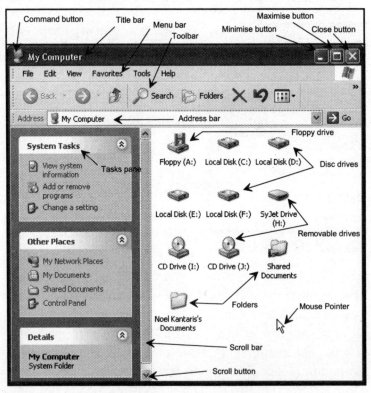

Fig. 1.8 The My Computer Screen.

Each application, and some documents you choose to work with, open and use separate windows to run in. Although every window has some common elements, not all windows use all of these elements. An application window is easily opened by either double-clicking its icon on the Desktop, or clicking its name on one of the cascaded menus resulting from clicking the *start* button. When a program is running, an icon is placed on the Taskbar (more about this later).

Although multiple application or document windows can be displayed simultaneously, only one is the active window and displays on the top of any other non-active windows. Title bars of non-active windows appear with a lighter shade than that of the active one, as shown in Fig. 1.9 below (here **My Computer** is the active one).

Fig. 1.9 Simultaneous Display of Running Applications.

The typical window is subdivided into several areas which have the following functions:

Area	*Function*
Command button	Left-clicking on this icon (see upper-left corner of the **My Computer** window in Fig. 1.8), displays the pull-down Control menu which can be used to control the window. It includes commands for restoring, moving, sizing, minimising, maximising, and closing the window.
Title bar	The bar at the top of a window which displays the application name and the name of the current document.
Minimise button	Left-clicking this button stores an application as an icon on the Taskbar. Clicking on such an icon will restore the window.
Maximise button	Left-clicking this button fills the screen with the active window. When that happens, the Maximise button changes to a Restore Down button which can be used to restore the window to its former size.

Close button

The extreme top right button ☒ that you click to close a window.

Menu bar

The bar below the Title bar which allows you to choose from several menu options. Clicking on a menu item displays the pull-down menu associated with that item. The options listed in the Menu bar depend on the specific application.

Toolbar

A bar of icons that you click to carry out some common actions.

Address bar

Shows the location of the current folder, or the URL (Uniform Resource Locator) of the new Web page to go to next.

Scroll bars/buttons

The bars/buttons on the extreme right and bottom of each window (or pane within a window) that contain a scroll box/button. Clicking on these allows you to see parts of a document that might not be visible in that size window.

Mouse pointer

The arrow which appears when the pointer is placed over menus, scroll bars, buttons, and folder lists.

Tasks

These change according to the function of the activated application. For example, if you activate My Computer, the Tasks refer to the System; you can view system information, add or remove programs, or change a setting. If you activate My Documents, the Tasks refer to files and folders; you can make a new folder, publish this folder to the Web, or share it with other users.

Other Places

The list shown under this heading also changes according to the function of the activated application. For example, if you activate My Computer, the list refers to activities related to it, such as My Network Places, My Documents, Shared Documents, and Control Panel. If you activate My Documents, the list refers to activities related to it, such as Desktop, Shared Documents, My Computer, and My Network Places.

Details

Gives details of the displayed Task.

Activity Related Tasks

Fig. 1.10 shows activity related Tasks. Here we have selected the **My Pictures** folder and, as you can see, the Picture Tasks and File and Folder Tasks menu lists change to reflect the current activity.

Fig. 1.10 Activity Related Tasks.

For example, from here you can view your pictures as a slide show, print a selected picture, etc., or rename, move, or delete a selected picture file. This allows you to reach easily and quickly related activities for the selected object (more about this later). Your pictures might be different to the ones above, but to see them in the shown form, use the **View**, **Thumbnails** menu command.

The Mouse Pointers

Windows has many different mouse pointers, with the most common illustrated below, which it uses for its various functions. When a program is initially started up probably the first you will see is the hourglass, which turns into an upward pointing hollow arrow. Some of the other shapes, as shown below, depend on the type of work you are doing at the time.

    The hourglass which displays when you are waiting while performing a function.

    The arrow which appears when the pointer is placed over menus, scrolling bars, and buttons.

    The I-beam which appears in normal text areas of the screen.

    The large 4-headed arrow which appears after choosing the Control, Move/Size command(s) for moving or sizing windows.

    The double arrows which appear when over the border of a window, used to drag the side and alter the size of the window.

    The Help hand which appears in the help windows, and is used to access 'hypertext' type links.

Windows applications, such as word processors, spreadsheets and databases, can have additional mouse pointers which facilitate the execution of selected commands, such as highlighting text or defining areas.

Using the Help System

To obtain help in Windows XP, click the *start* button, then click the **Help and Support** menu option which opens the main Help window, shown in Fig. 1.11 below.

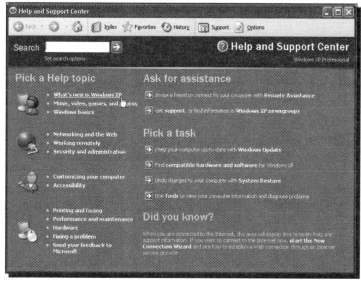

Fig. 1.11 The Windows XP Help and Support Center.

The **Pick a Help topic** option gives you off-line help on various listed topics, while the **Ask for assistance** topics require connection to the Internet, as do the first two options under **Pick a task**. It might be worth your while spending some time here investigating the various options available to you. If you are new to Windows, you might like to have a look at the 'What's new in Windows XP' option.

With all options you get a 'Search' facility, and with all but the 'start a New Connection Wizard' under the **Did you know?** option you are presented with an extraordinary number of hypertext links to various topics. Clicking such a hypertext link, can open up a further list of hypertext links until you home onto the specific subject you are searching for.

The Search facility gives you access to a very powerful individual word search of the Help system, as shown in Fig. 1.12 below. For example, if you wanted to know something about e-mail, type the word *e-mail* in the Search box and click the ⊡ button to have Windows display almost everything there is to know about e-mail.

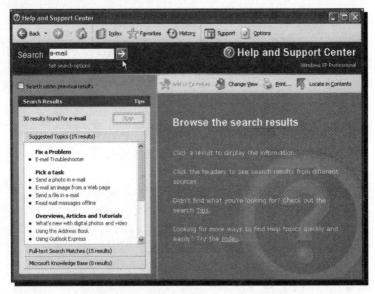

Fig. 1.12 Using the Help Search Facility.

The last item under each Search screen's **Browse the search results** statement is always the **Index** link. Clicking this link, opens up a Help index facility and typing the first few letters of a word in its input box homes onto the available topics in the list. Selecting one and clicking the **Display** button opens its help page on that item. Try it.

Exiting Windows XP

To exit Windows, click the *start* button and select the **Turn Off Computer** option, as shown in Fig. 1.13.

Fig. 1.13 The Lower Part of the Start Menu.

This opens an additional box, shown in Fig. 1.14 below.

Fig. 1.14 The Turn Off Computer
Dialogue Box.

From here you can either put your computer in a **Stand by** mode, **Turn Off** the computer, or **Restart** it. The **Stand by** mode is used to save power by turning off your monitor and/or hard disc after a specified time interval (see also Chapter 9, page 196). Selecting the **Turn Off** option, exits all the open programs, carries out any file saves you require and then tells you when it is safe to switch off your computer. The **Restart** option is used if you want to clear the memory settings and restart Windows XP, or if you have a dual boot system to start the other operating system.

Note: Unlike previous versions of Windows where this was the only way that you should end a session, with Window XP you can just switch off your computer - the **Turn Off** the computer procedure will then be carried out automatically.

***

In the next chapter we discuss the Windows environment with its common toolbar buttons, menu bar options, dialogue boxes, and Taskbar buttons so that you can find your way around your programs and data. We then show you how to manipulate windows on the desktop by sizing, moving, minimising, maximising and displaying them in different ways on the screen.

2

The Windows Environment

You must have noticed by now that the **My Computer**, and **My Documents** folders, to mention but a few, have a Toolbar with browser-style forwards and backwards arrows similar to the **Internet Explorer** which is bundled with Windows XP. The **My Computer** window is shown in Fig. 2.1 below.

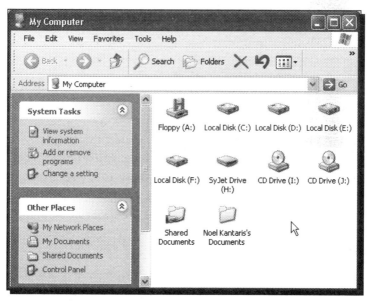

Fig. 2.1 The Toolbar of a Windows Application.

Note that for the above display we have used the **View** button on the Toolbar and selected the **Icons** option.

For the display in Fig. 2.2, we chose the **Details** option. Highlighting an item, in whichever display option you operate, gives you information about that item.

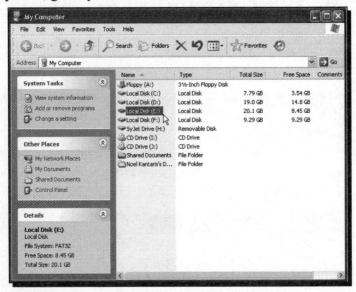

Fig. 2.2 The Details View Option.

Additional information can be obtained by right-clicking

an item such as a drive, a folder or a file and selecting **Properties** from the drop-down menu. In Fig. 2.3 we show the Properties box of a local disc which displays visually its capacity. You can also find out what maintenance tools are available by clicking the appropriate tab.

Fig. 2.3 The Properties Box.

The Common Toolbar Buttons

Returning to the common user interface Toolbar, apart from the default buttons appearing on it, there are several others which can be added to invoke extra facilities. To do this, use the **View, Toolbars, Customize** command to display the screen shown in Fig. 2.4 below.

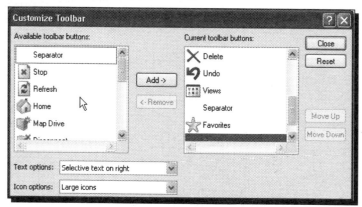

Fig. 2.4 The Customize Toolbar Dialogue Box.

To place an additional button on the Toolbar, select it in the left pane, and press the **Add** button. Its place on the Toolbar depends on the position of the focus in the right pane. Once a button has been added on a Toolbar, it will also appear on the Toolbar of all other program applications that use the same common user interface.

Some applications or utilities display a '?' button on the right end of their title bar as shown here to the left (see also Fig. 2.4) Clicking this button changes the mouse pointer from its usual inclined arrow shape to the 'What's this?' shape. Pointing with this to an object in the window and clicking, opens a Help topic.

The various buttons on the common interface Toolbar have the following functions:

Button	*Function*
Back ▾	Go back to the previous display.
➔ ▾	Go Forward to the next display.
🔼	Go up one step in the hierarchical tree structure of the filing system.
Search	Search for folders and files, for computers or people or the Internet.
Folders	Replace the Tasks pane with a hierarchical tree structure of your filing system.
✕	Delete selected items.
↩	Undo last command.
▦ ▾	Select a different view for displaying your files and folders.
Favorites	Show your favourite links to Web sites on the Internet or to folders on your hard disc.

The Menu Bar Options

Each window's menu bar option has associated with it a pull-down sub-menu. To activate a menu option, point to it with the mouse to highlight it and click the left mouse button. As the mouse pointer is moved onto each of the sub-menu options it highlights it. To activate a sub-menu option, highlight it and click the left mouse button.

The sub-menu of the **View** option of the My Documents window, is shown in Fig. 2.5 below.

Fig. 2.5 Menu Bar Options.

Items on the pull-down sub-menu which are marked with an arrow to their right, as shown here, open up additional options when selected, as shown on the My Documents window of Fig. 2.5.

The items on the menu bar of a specific application might be different from the ones shown here. However, almost all Windows XP system applications offer the following options:

File   Produces a pull-down menu of mainly file related tasks, which allow you, amongst other options, to **rename**, **move**, **copy**, **publish on the Web**, **e-mail**, **print**, or **close** a file or folder.

Edit   Gives access to the most common editing tasks which can be applied on selected items, such as **cut**, **copy** and **paste**, **copy** or **move** such items to a folder, or **select all** files or folders.

View   Gives you control over what you see on the screen. For example, selecting the **Toolbars**, **Status bar**, or **Explorer bar** options checks these options and allows their display (selecting them once more removes the check mark and toggles them off). Files can be displayed as **thumbnails**, by their **titles**, **icons**, as **lists** or you can display their **details**.

Favorites Allows you to **add** and **organise** useful URL addresses, customise **links**, or access various pre-set **media** addresses on the Internet.

Tools   Allows you to **map** or **disconnect** network drives, and set **folder options**.

Help   Activates the **help and support centre**, or opens a window and displays basic system information.

Note: Having activated a menu, whether from the menu bar or a right-click, you can close it without taking any further action by simply left-clicking the mouse pointer somewhere else on the screen, or by simply pressing the <Esc> key.

Dialogue Boxes

Three periods after a sub-menu option or command, means that a dialogue box will open when the option or command is selected. A dialogue box is used for the insertion of additional information, such as the name of a file.

To see a dialogue box, click the *start* button and select the **My Computer** menu option. Next, select **Tools** on the menu bar of the displayed window and **Folder Options** from its sub-menu. This opens the Folder Options with its General tab selected. In Fig. 2.6 on the next page we show this dialogue box with its View tab selected so that you can see two different types of option lists.

When a dialogue box opens, the <Tab> key can be used to move the dotted rectangle (known as the focus) from one field to another. Alternatively you can use the mouse to left-click directly the desired field.

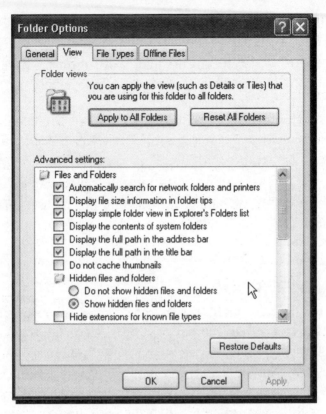

Fig. 2.6 The Folder Options Dialogue Box.

Some dialogue boxes (such as the one shown in Fig. 2.6) contain List boxes which show a column of available choices. If there are more choices than can be seen in the area provided, use the scroll bars to reveal them. Such dialogue boxes may contain Check boxes, as shown to the left, which offer a list of features you can switch on or off. Selected options show a tick in the box against the option name.

Another type of option available in this dialogue box is the Option button (sometimes called Radio button) with a list of mutually exclusive items. The default choice is marked with a black dot against its name, while unavailable options are dimmed.

Another type of List box may display a column of document files. To select a single file from such a List box, either double-click the file, or use the arrow keys to highlight the file and press <Enter>. Again, if there are more files than can be seen in the area provided, use the scroll bars to reveal them.

Other dialogue boxes may contain groups of options within a field. In such cases, you can use the arrow keys to move from one option to another. Having selected an option or typed in information in a text box, you must press a command button, such as the **OK**, **Cancel** or **Apply** button (unavailable options or command buttons are dimmed), or choose from additional options. To select the **OK** button with the mouse, simply point and left-click, while with the keyboard, you must first press the <Tab> key until the focus moves to the required button, and then press the <Enter> key.

To cancel a dialogue box, either press the **Cancel** button, or the <Esc> key enough times to close the dialogue box and then the menu system.

Note: At this stage it might be a good time to change the default settings under the **View** tab of Fig. 2.6 by unchecking the **Hide extensions for known file types** option. Doing so could alert you to rogue and potentially lethal e-mail attachments.

Exercises

In the following exercises we will look at the System Properties and make certain choices using **My Computer**, and add a button to the Standard Buttons bar. To do this, follow the instructions below:

1. To display the System Properties dialogue box do the following:

   • Left-click the *start* button, then right-click the **My Computer** entry on the *start* menu, and select **Properties**.

   • The displayed Properties dialogue box should look similar to the one shown in Fig. 2.7 below.

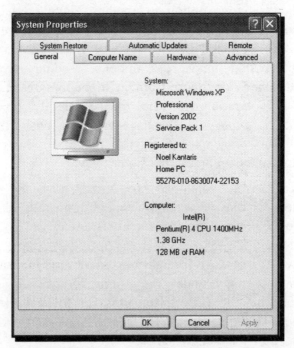

Fig. 2.7 The System Properties Dialogue Box.

- Next, click the Automatic Updates tab and make sure that the 'Keep my computer up to date' box is checked and that under 'Settings' the first radio button is selected. In this way you will remain in total control of automatic updates when you connect to the Internet in the future.

- Press **OK** to make changes.

2. To add a button to the Standard Buttons bar, do the following:

  - Left-click the *start* button, then left-click **My Computer** on the displayed menu list.

  - On the displayed **My Computer** window use the **View, Toolbars, Customize** menu command to display the Customize Toolbar dialogue box shown in Fig. 2.8 below.

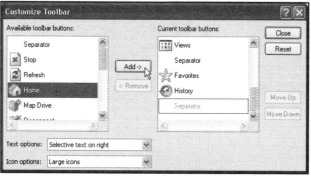

Fig. 2.8 The Customize Toolbar Dialogue Box.

  - Left-click the **Home** entry under the **Available toolbar buttons** list to select it, as shown above, then click the **Add** button to add it to the **Current toolbar buttons**, then click the **Close** button.

Taskbar Buttons

At the bottom of the Desktop screen is the Taskbar. It contains the *start* button which, as we have seen, can be used to quickly start a program. Later on we will discuss how we can search for a file, and how to get Help.

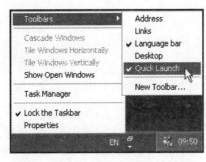

Before we go any further, right-click an empty part of the Taskbar, point to the **Toolbars** option which displays the sub-menu, shown on the right in Fig. 2.9, and left-click the **Quick Launch** entry.

Fig. 2.9 Quick Launch Activation.

This displays three icons next to the *start* button; left-clicking one of these, launches its application. In order of appearance they have the following functions:

Launch the Internet Explorer Browser.

Show Desktop.

Launch Windows Media Player.

When you open a program, or a window, a button for it is placed on the Taskbar, as shown in Fig. 2.10 below.

Fig. 2.10 The Windows Taskbar.

You can left-click your mouse on this button to make this the active program, or window, which displays in a darker shade of blue on the Taskbar. So, now you can always see what windows you have open, which is the active one, and quickly switch between them.

As more buttons are placed on the Taskbar their size shrinks slightly, but up to a point. After that, common entries are grouped together with a number indicating the number of open windows. To see details relating to a grouped button, left-click it to open a list of components, as shown in Fig. 2.11.

Another interesting Taskbar menu option is **Properties** (Fig. 2.12). This allows you to change the Taskbar and *start* menu options.

Fig. 2.11 Grouped Taskbar Entries.

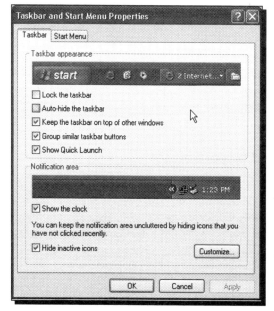

Fig. 2.12 The Taskbar and Start Menu Properties box.

To the far right of the Taskbar you can also see displayed the current time, the Windows Messenger, the Options,

the Restore and the Language icons. Moving the mouse pointer over the clock will display the date. Double-clicking the clock, opens the Date/Time Properties box, shown in Fig. 2.13, so that you can make changes, if necessary.

Fig. 2.13 Date and Time Properties Dialogue Box.

Manipulating Windows

To use any Windows program effectively, you will need to be able to manipulate a series of windows, to select which one is to be active, to move them, or change their size, so that you can see all the relevant parts of each one. What follows is a short discussion on how to achieve this.

Changing the Active Window

To select the active window amongst those displayed on the screen (these will only be displayed on the screen simultaneously if their Restore Down button has been left-clicked), point to it and click the left mouse button, or, if the one you want to activate is not visible, click its icon on the Taskbar.

Sizing a Window

You can change the size of a window with the mouse by first moving the window so that the side you want to change is visible, then moving the mouse pointer to the edge of the window or corner so that it changes to a two-headed arrow, then dragging the two-headed arrow in the direction you want that side or corner to move.

Moving Windows and Dialogue Boxes

To move a window (or a dialogue box) with the mouse, point to its title bar (see Fig. 2.14), and drag it until it is where you want it to be on the screen, then release the mouse button. This can only be achieved if the window does not occupy the full screen.

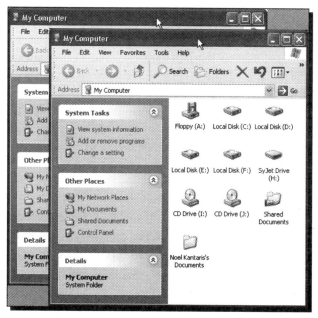

Fig. 2.14 Moving a Window with the Mouse.

Minimising and Maximising Windows

To minimise a window into a Taskbar icon (to temporarily free desktop space) left-click the Minimise button (the negative sign in the upper-right corner of the window), shown in Fig. 2.15.

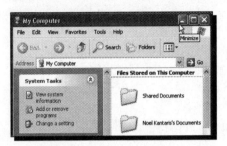

Fig. 2.15 Minimising a Window.

To maximise a window so that it fills the entire screen, left-click the Maximise button (the rectangle in the upper-right corner of the window.

An application which has been minimised or maximised

can be returned to its original size and position on the screen by either clicking on its Taskbar icon to expand it to a window, or clicking on the Restore Down button of the maximised window, to reduce it to its former size.

Closing a Window

A document window can be closed at any time to save

screen space and memory. To do this, left-click the Close (X) button shown here. If you try to close a window of an application document, such as that of a word processor, in which you have made changes since the last time you saved it, you will get a warning in the form of a dialogue box asking confirmation prior to closing it. This safeguards against loss of information.

Exercises

In the following exercises we will create a new folder, name it, and rename it. To do this, follow the instructions below:

3. To practise what we have described above do the following:

   - Open the three applications **My Computer**, **My Documents**, and **My Pictures** from the start menu, in that order.

   - Make **My Computer** the active window by left-clicking it.

   - Re-size the active window by dragging one of its sides to make it bigger.

   - Move the active window so that its title bar touches the top of the screen.

   - Minimise each open window into a Taskbar icon by successively left-clicking each window's Minimise button (the negative sign in the upper-right corner of a window).

   - Left-click the **My Computer** Taskbar icon to maximise its window and make it the active window, then left-click the Close button (the X sign in the upper-right corner of the window) to exit the program.

   - Repeat the last two steps to close the remaining two programs.

Do not be afraid if you make mistakes - you will only learn from them!

Windows Display Arrangement

In Windows and most Windows application programs,

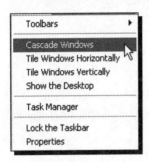

Fig. 2.16 The Taskbar Shortcut Menu.

you can display multiple windows in both tiled and cascaded (overlapping) forms - the choice being a matter of balance between personal preference and the type of work you are doing at the time. If you want to organise these automatically, right-click on an empty part of the Taskbar which opens the menu shown in Fig. 2.16.

Below we show two forms of windows display; the **Cascade Windows** option (Fig. 2.17) and the **Tile Windows Vertically** option (Fig. 2.18).

Fig. 2.17 Windows Displayed in Cascade Form.

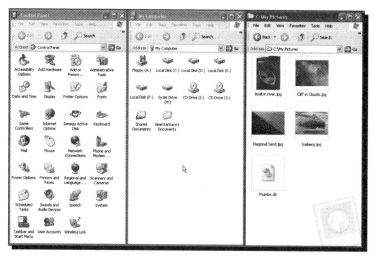

Fig. 2.18 Windows Displayed in Vertical Tile Form.

As we have discussed earlier, the size of these windows can be changed, hence you might have to alter their size to display exactly what is displayed in Fig. 2.17 and Fig. 2.18.

Exercises

4. To practise what we have described above do the following:

- Open **My Computer**, and **Control Panel** from the *start* menu.

- Display their windows in horizontal form by right-clicking an empty area of the Taskbar and selecting **Tile Windows Horizontally** from the displayed shortcut menu.

- Next display the two windows in vertical form to see which version you prefer.

***

In the next chapter we discuss how to create a new folder, how to name it and rename it, how to search your computer for specific files (or folders) and copy or move them into the new folder. We then show you how to create application shortcuts, followed by how to send files or folders to specific destinations. These skills are required if you want to keep your documents, pictures, and music files in some sort of organised manner so that you can find them later quickly and easily. Finally, we discuss the Recycle Bin in which deleted files and folders are kept until you decide whether you want them after all or delete them for good.

3

Working with Files and Folders

In this chapter we discuss the skills you will need to keep your data organised so that you can easily find your documents, pictures or music files at a later stage. Windows provides you with the means to keep such files in folders which you can create for the purpose, copy files into them, or even delete unwanted files from them. Folders, which can also contain other folders, are kept on your hard disc which is not dissimilar to the idea of a filing cabinet, if one is to use an analogy.

It is possible, of course, that you might have more than one fixed hard disc (as we do - see Fig. 1.8), or that you might have one or more removable hard discs attached to your system. Whether you have such additional *filing cabinets* or not, is not important as the skills required to keep one organised can also be applied to the others.

Windows provides you, by default, with one folder called **My Documents** which can be accessed from the *start* menu. In this folder there are other folders such as **My Pictures** and **My Music** also accessible from the *start* menu. In what follows, we will carry on with this structured tradition, so that folders we create are also contained within the **My Documents** folder. In this way, when you left-click **My Documents** on the *start* menu, all the other folders will be available to you.

Creating a New Folder

In what follows we will create a new folder, name it, and rename it. To do this, follow the instructions below:

To create a new folder within, say **My Documents**, do the following:

- Left-click the *start* button to display its menu.

- Left-click **My Documents** at the top of the right column of the menu to display Fig. 3.1 below (in your case the contents of this will be different).

- Point to the **Make a new folder** entry on the **Tasks** pane and when it changes to a hand, as shown in Fig. 3.1 below, left-click it.

Fig. 3.1 Creating a New Folder.

To Name a newly created folder, do the following:

- When Windows creates a new folder it places it at the end of the list of existing folders and names it **New Folder**, highlighting its name and waiting for you to name it, as shown here.

- Type a name, say, Photos, which replaces the default name given to it by Windows. If this doesn't happen, don't worry, you must have clicked the left mouse button an extra time which fixes the default name (see below how to rename it)

To rename a folder or a file, do the following:

Method 1

- Left-click the folder or file you want to rename to select it.

- Left-clicking it once more will display the insertion pointer within its name. Type a different name to replace the existing one.

Method 2

- Left-click the folder or file you want to rename to select it (in this example we chose a folder).

- Left-click the **Rename this folder** entry on the **Tasks** menu which causes the insertion pointer to be displayed within its name. Type a different name to replace the existing one.

Searching for Files and Folders

In order to demonstrate how to select files (or folders) we need to already have some files, common to both us and you, that we can work with. To do this, we will search our hard disc for picture files hopefully provided to all Windows XP users.

To search for files, left-click the *start* menu and select the **Search** option. This opens the Search Dialogue box, the left panel of which is shown in Fig. 3.2. Next, click the **All files and folders** entry in the Tasks pane (as shown in Fig. 3.2).

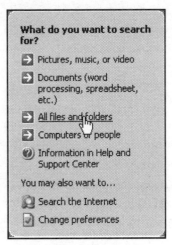

What do you want to search for?

➔ Pictures, music, or video

➔ Documents (word processing, spreadsheet, etc.)

➔ All files and folders

➔ Computers or people

⍰ Information in Help and Support Center

You may also want to...

🔍 Search the Internet

☑ Change preferences

Fig. 3.2 Specifying Type of Search.

You now need to specify the name (or part of it - see next page) of the item you are searching for and the drive you want to search (in this case the drive where Windows is installed on your PC), as shown in Fig. 3.3.

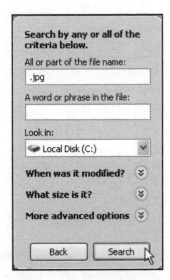

Search by any or all of the criteria below.

All or part of the file name:

.jpg

A word or phrase in the file:

Look in:

Local Disk (C:)

When was it modified? ⊗

What size is it? ⊗

More advanced options ⊗

Back   Search

Fig. 3.3 Specifying the Item and Drive for a Search.

Filename Convention

File names can be as long as 255 characters, including spaces, but keeping them short is a very good idea as long names can result in typographical errors. However, the name must not contain any of the following keyboard characters:

| / | \ | > | < | * | ? | " | | | : | ; |

A filename can also include a file extension which is the optional suffix following the period in a filename. Windows uses this to identify the application program that created it.

For example, if you were using Microsoft Word to create, say, a letter, when you save it under the filename **My letter** the program automatically adds the extension **.doc** to it, so now the filename appears as **My letter.doc**. In this way Windows knows that this file was created by Microsoft Word. Double-clicking such a filename causes Windows to load Microsoft Word first then open the letter ready for any changes you might want to make to it.

Below we list some of the popular filename extensions.

.bak	a backup file
.exe	an executable file
.hlp	a hypertext help file
.html	a hypertext markup language file
.jpeg or .jpg	a graphic format file
.rtf	a rich text format file
.sys	a system file
.tmp or .temp	a temporary file
.txt	a basic text file
.wav	a waveform of a soundbite.

Search Results

Going back to our search criteria, we specified in Fig. 3.3 that part of the filename we want to search for is .jpg which indicates we are interested in graphic files. Left-clicking the **Search** button, produces the list of files shown in Fig. 3.4 below.

Fig. 3.4 Search Results for .jpg Files.

What is displayed above is a fraction of the total files found by this particular search. You might have to scroll down a bit to find what appears above, which are part of the contents of the **Windows\Web\Wallpaper** folder.

In what follows we will use these files to demonstrate file management such as selecting, copying, sending, deleting, etc. You could, of course, use your own choice of files, but the ones we are using here are common to all computers running Windows XP. That is why we chose to use these files in particular.

Selecting Files and Folders

What we demonstrate below with files could also be done with folders, or a mixture of files and folders within any folder. Here we use the files in the **Wallpaper** folder.

To select several objects, or icons, you have three options:

- If they form a contiguous list, as shown in Fig. 3.5 below, left-click the first in the list, then with the <Shift> key depressed, click the last in the list.

Fig. 3.5 Selecting Items in a Folder.

- To select random objects hold the <Ctrl> key down and left-click them, one by one.

- To select all the items in a window use the **Edit**, **Select All** menu command, or the <Ctrl+A> keystrokes.

To cancel a selection, click in an empty area of the window.

Copying or Moving Files and Folders

When you *copy* a file or folder to somewhere else, the original version of the folder or file is not altered or removed, but when you *move* a folder or file to a new location, the original is actually deleted.

To copy selected items into a target folder, right-click the selected items and choose the **Copy** option from the shortcut menu as shown in Fig. 3.6 below.

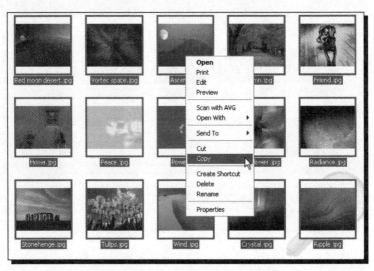

Fig. 3.6 Copying Selected Files to the Clipboard.

The selected files are then copied to the Windows Clipboard which is a temporary storage area of memory where text and graphics are stored with the Windows **Cut** and **Copy** actions.

All you need to do now is navigate to the **My Photos** folder, double-click it to open it, right-click it and select the **Paste** option from the displayed shortcut menu.

In Fig. 3.7 below, we show on the same screen dump the action to be taken and the result you will get from that action. For you, of course, these will display separately.

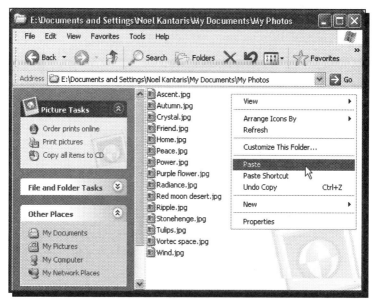

Fig. 3.7 Pasting Items from the Clipboard.

The contents of the folder above are shown in **List** view. To see them as displayed in Fig. 3.6 use the **View**, **Thumbnails** menu command.

To move selected items into a target folder choose the **Cut** option from the shortcut menu (see Fig. 3.6). This removes the selected files from their current place and copies them to the Windows Clipboard so that you can **Paste** then into the target folder.

The method described above for copying or moving files and folders is not the only one available (another way is to use the drag and drop method or the Tasks Pane options), but in this case it is the most convenient one.

Sending Files and Folders

A very useful feature of Windows is the ability to quickly send files and folders to specific destinations.

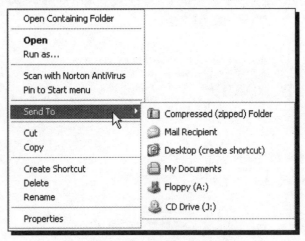

Fig. 3.8 Sending Folders and Files.

As we have seen earlier, right-clicking selected folders, or files, will open the menu shown in Fig. 3.8. Selecting the **Send To** option opens the list of available destinations. In your case these are bound to be different. Selecting the **Floppy (A)** option will copy any selected folders and files to a removable disc in the (A:) drive.

It is easy to add more locations to the **Send To** menu, as it is controlled by the contents of the **SendTo** folder, which is itself in the **Windows** folder. However, the **SendTo** folder is hidden by default, so if you use the *start*, **Search** command, you may not find it. To make it visible, start **My Computer**, then use the **Tools, Folder Options** command, click the View tab and finally click the **Show hidden files and folders** option.

To add a destination to the **Send To** menu use **My Computer** to do the following:

- Click the **Documents and Settings** folder on the drive where Windows XP is installed.

- Double-click the folder of a specific user.

- Double-click the **SendTo** folder.

- Use the **File, New, Shortcut** command as shown in Fig. 3.9 below.

Fig. 3.9 Adding a Shortcut to the SendTo Folder.

- Finally, follow the instructions on your screen.

Exercises

To practice what we have discussed so far, do the following:

1. Add both **My Photos** and **My Pictures** as a destination to the **Send To** menu, as described on the previous page. The modified **Send To** menu should now look similar to that of Fig. 3.10.

Fig. 3.10 The Modified Send To Menu.

2. Repeat the search for .jpg files as discussed earlier and copy any images from the **Wallpaper** folder missing from our previous selection into **My Photos**. If you followed our instructions to the letter, there should be four more images that you could use; one above our selection shown in Fig. 3.6, and three below (provided the width of your display window was five images across). Since you are selecting non-contiguous images, hold the <Ctrl> key down and left-click them one by one.

3. Copy a selection of images from **My Photos** into **My Pictures** using the **Send To** shortcut menu option.

   If you decide to rename an item in the **Send To** menu, use **My Computer** and navigate to the **SendTo** folder, via **Documents and Settings/User** folder, right-click the item which you want to rename, and select the **Rename** command from the displayed shortcut menu.

Creating Shortcuts

With Windows XP you can put a shortcut to any program or document on your desktop or in any folder. Shortcuts are quick ways to get to the items you use often; they save you having to dig into cascade menus to access them.

One program that you might want to access quickly, to say write a quick letter, is **WordPad**, so we will step you through the process of finding and placing a shortcut to it on the desktop.

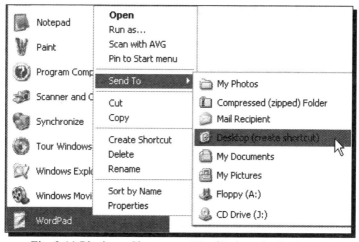

Fig. 3.11 Placing a Shortcut to WordPad on the Desktop.

As WordPad is in the **Accessories** folder, to locate it use the *start*, **All Programs**, **Accessories** menu option. Next, highlight **WordPad**, right-click it, and select **Send To**, **Desktop (create shortcut)** option, as shown in Fig. 3.11.

Double-clicking such a shortcut icon on the desktop will be easier and quicker than digging deep into the cascade menus to open the program.

Deleting Files or Folders

The operations described here must only be carried out on the files held in the **Photos** folder, unless you really want to delete specific items from another folder.

To delete or remove items (files or folders), first highlight them, and then either select the **Delete the selected items** entry in the Tasks pane, press the <Del> key on the keyboard, or press the **Delete** button on the Toolbar, shown here, or use the **File, Delete** command from the window menu bar.

All of these methods open the confirmation box shown in Fig. 3.12 which gives you the chance to abort the operation by selecting **No**.

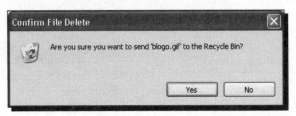

Fig. 3.12 The Delete File Warning Dialogue Box.

To delete folders, follow the same procedure as for files. A similar dialogue box to the one in Fig 3.12 will be displayed. The only difference is that the word 'File' is replaced by the word 'Folder'. To carry on with the deletion in either case, select **Yes**.

Now is the time to delete two image files from our **Photos** folder (any files will do). Do carry out this suggestion as we need to demonstrate what happens to deleted items when we discuss the **Recycle Bin**.

The Recycle Bin

As you can see from the message boxes on the previous page, by default all files or folders deleted from a hard disc, are actually placed in a holding folder named the **Recycle Bin**.

If you open the **Recycle Bin**, by double-clicking its desktop icon, shown here, you will see that it is just a special folder. It lists all the files, folders, icons and shortcuts that have been deleted from fixed drives since it was last emptied, as shown in Fig. 3.13. To see the display as it appears below, use the **View**, **List** menu option.

Fig. 3.13 The Recycle Bin Folder Showing Deleted Files.

Windows keeps a record of the original locations of the deleted files, so that it can restore them if necessary. To restore or delete all the items in the **Recycle Bin**, click the **Restore all items** or **Empty the Recycle Bin** option in the Tasks pane.

To restore or delete specific files or folders from the **Recycle Bin**, first select them then use the appropriate Tasks pane entry. Choosing **Restore the selected items** will restore the selected files to the folder they were originally in, even if you have deleted that folder.

Clicking the **Delete** icon on the Toolbar, removes the selected items from the **Recycle Bin**. To save disc space, every now and then, open the **Recycle Bin** and delete unwanted files or folders.

Exercises

In the following exercises you will practise deleting files and their folder, before restoring them to their original location. We will use **My Photos** and its contents for this exercises, therefore, if you haven't done so already, create it and copy the recommended files into it before going on.

4. To delete files and folders, do the following:

  * Select five non-contiguous images held in **My Photos**, then press the <Delete> keyboard key. In the Confirm File Delete dialogue box, click **Yes**.

  * Next select the **My Photos** folder and delete it.

5. To restore files and folders, do the following:

  * Double-click the **Recycle Bin** on your desktop.

  * Left-click one of the image files to select it and click **Restore this item** on the Tasks menu. Note that the file is restored in its containing folder

  * Left-click the **My Photos** folder to select it and click the **Restore this item** on the Tasks menu. Note the warning message displayed on the screen.

Other Image Folder Views

In Fig. 3.14 below, we display the contents of the **My Photos** folder as **Thumbnails** with one image selected and its shortcut (right-click) menu also shown.

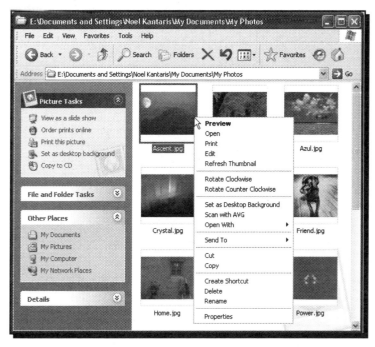

Fig. 3.14 The Pictures Folder Displayed in Thumbnail View.

Images can be arranged by name, size, type, etc., from the **View** menu, or can be previewed, rotated, set as desktop background, or opened in a variety of imaging programs, from its shortcut menu, as shown in Fig. 3.14 above.

You can also use the Tasks menu to view images as a slide show, set a selected image as a desktop background, print a selected image, or copy selected images to a CD.

Previewing an Image

If you double-click an image or select **Preview** from its shortcut menu, then that image is displayed enlarged in the Windows **Picture and Fax Viewer**, as shown in Fig. 3.15 below.

Fig. 3.15 The Windows Picture and Fax Viewer.

Note the buttons at the bottom of the screen. You can use these to navigate through your pictures folder, select the viewing size, view the pictures in your folder as a slide show, zoom in or out, rotate the image, and generally carry out certain housekeeping functions, including the opening of the picture in Microsoft Photo Editor so that you can edit it.

The Windows **Picture and Fax Viewer** can of course be used with other image documents including scanned pictures, digital camera photos or fax documents.

The Filmstrip View

To see your photos in another interesting display, use the **View**, **Filmstrip** command. To get the full benefit of this view, you need to increase the size of the displayed window to at least ¾ of the size of your screen. The result should look similar to that in Fig. 3.16 below.

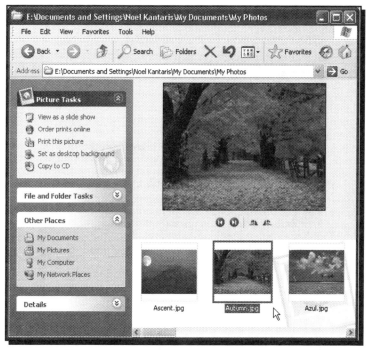

Fig. 3.16 Photos Displayed in Filmstrip View.

As each image is selected, an enlarged view of it displays above the filmstrip. The four buttons below the enlarged view can be used to navigate to the previous or the next image, and to rotate the selected image clockwise or anticlockwise.

Copying Files or Folders to a CD

To copy files or folders to a CD, you will need a recordable compact disc (CD-R) or a rewritable compact disc (CD-RW) and a CD recorder. To start the process, insert a blank recordable or rewritable CD in the CD recorder, then do the following:

- Use **My Computer** to locate and select the files or folder you want to copy to the CD. Make sure that the selected files or folder contents do not exceed the CD's capacity (650 MB for a standard CD).

- Click the **Copy to CD** Tasks menu option, as shown in Fig. 3.17.

Fig. 3.17 Copying Selected Files to a CD.

The copying process is then started and you will be notified when it is completed. This method is excellent for making backups of your important data.

However, should the data you are trying to copy on a CD be large graphical images obtained from, say, a digital camera or a scanner, then it might be a good idea to compress such images before attempting to copy them onto a CD, as discussed below.

Compressing Files and Folders

Compressing files and folders allows you to greatly increase the storage capacity of your hard disc and increases the amount of data you can copy on a single CD. As an example we will use data held on one of our computers, in a folder called **My Scans** which is just over 50 MB in size, and send it to a compressed folder that we will create.

Fig. 3.18 Creating a Zipped Folder.

To start the process, open the drive or folder in which you want to create a compressed folder (we chose to create it within **My Documents**), then use the **File, New** menu command, and select the **Compressed (zipped) Folder** option from the drop-down menu (see Fig. 3.18).

The created folder has the extension **.zip** and you must retain this when renaming it. We renamed our folder **My Scans.zip**. We then opened **My Computer** and located the original **My Scans** folder which, again, in our case is to be found in **My Documents**, then used the **Edit, Select All** menu command and dragged the highlighted files into the newly renamed folder, as shown in Fig. 3.19.

Fig. 3.19 Dragging a File into a Compressed Folder.

Releasing the mouse button displays the Compressing dialogue box shown in Fig. 3.20 below.

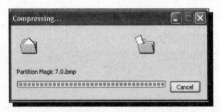

Fig. 3.20 Compressing a File.

You can send other files and folders into the compressed folder by dragging them onto it. Selected files are then compressed one at time before they are moved into the folder, while the contents of the dragged folders are also compressed.

To find out the size of the folder's contents before and after compression, double-click the compressed folder, use the **Edit, Select All** menu command, right-click on the highlighted files and select **Properties** from the drop-down menu to display the box in Fig. 3.21.

Fig. 3.21 Compressed File Properties.

Note that the size of the original 34 files is displayed as 52.164 MB, while its packed size as 40.546 MB. Some types of files compress even more. For example, the first four chapters of this book compress from 27.73 MB to 11.45 MB; a large enough compression ratio and worth exploiting.

You can open files and programs in a compressed folder by double-clicking them. If a program requires **.dll** (dynamic link library) or data files to run, then those files must first be extracted. To extract a file or folder from a compressed folder, simply drag it to its new location. To extract all files and folders within a compressed folder, right-click the folder and select **Extract All**. In the Extract

Wizard you can specify where you want these files and folders to be extracted to.

When you compress files or folders as explained earlier, the original files or folders remain on your hard disc. To remove such files and folders from the originating disc or folder you must delete them. Similarly, when you extract files or folders it leaves a copy of these in the compressed folder. To remove files and folders from a compressed folder you must delete them.

Exercises

In the following exercises use the contents of **My Photos** to:

6. Display the images as a slide show by doing the following:

   - Use the **View, Thumbnails** menu option to display the images as shown in Fig. 3.14.

   - Click the **View as a slide show** option on the **Tasks** menu. When you have had enough, press the <Esc> keyboard key to return to the **Thumbnails** view.

7. Rotate an image by doing the following:

   - Right-click the **Follow.jpg** image (the goldfish) and select **Preview** from the drop-down shortcut menu.

   - In the **Windows Picture and Fax Viewer**, first rotate the image by 180° so that the goldfish point in the opposite direction, before restoring them to their rightful direction by reversing the rotation.

4

Controlling your PC

You can control your PC primarily from the Windows Control Panel which provides a quick and easy way to change the hardware and software settings of your system.

The Windows Control Panel

To access the **Control Panel**, left-click the start button, then left-click the **Control Panel** entry on the displayed cascade menu, as shown in Fig. 4.1 below.

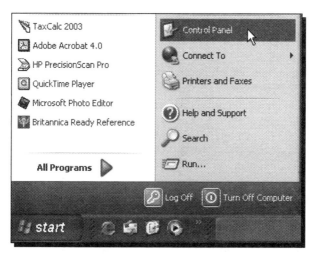

Fig. 4.1 The Control Panel Menu Option.

This opens the **Control Panel** window which displays either as shown in Fig. 4.2 (in Classic view) or Fig. 4.3 (in Category view).

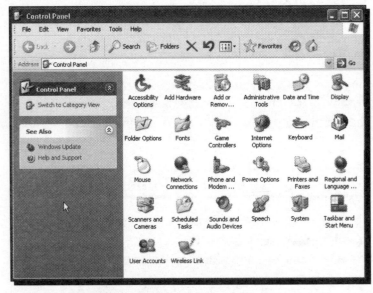

Fig. 4.2 The Control Panel Window.

To see the **Control Panel** in Category view, left-click the entry **Switch to Category View** on the left panel (pointed to here) to display Fig. 4.3.

Which view you choose to work with is a matter of preference. However, each option within the Category view displays an additional screen in which you are asked to **Pick a task** or **Pick a Control Panel icon**, which can be a bit confusing.

Fig. 4.3 The Control Panel Window in Category View.

From either of these views (we prefer the Classic view), you can add new hardware, add or remove programs, change the display type and its resolution, change the printer fonts, and change the keyboard repeat rate. Further, you can change the settings of your mouse, install and configure your printer(s), specify regional settings, such as the formatting of numbers and dates, and access a variety of system administrative tools. If your system is connected to the outside world or supports multimedia, then you can also configure it appropriately. All of these features control the environment in which the Windows application programs operate and you should become familiar with them.

Changing your Display

Windows XP required a minimum screen resolution of 800 by 600 pixels (picture elements). If your display is capable of higher resolution, you might like to increase it to, say, 1024 by 768 pixels, or higher. This will allow you to see a larger number of icons on a screen when a given application is activated. To achieve this, do the following:

- In the **Control Panel** window (Classic view), double-click the **Display** icon shown here.

- In the Display Properties dialogue box, click the Settings tab to display Fig. 4.4.

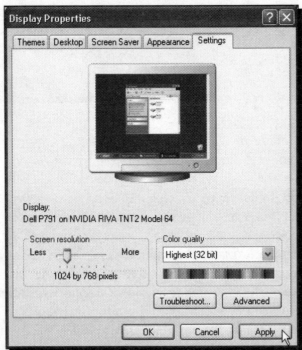

Fig. 4.4 The Settings Screen of the Display Properties.

For the new settings to take effect, click the **Apply** button. While the Display Properties dialogue box is open, you might like to explore the other available settings. For example:

- Click the Themes tab to change the looks of your active windows - best left as it is.

- Click the Desktop tab to change the background of your desktop, which by default was set to 'Bliss'. The first four background options are quite interesting, or you could select 'None' - best left as it is.

- Click the Screen Savers tab to select a different screen saver (Fig. 4.5) - you will be able to preview your selection before making a final choice.

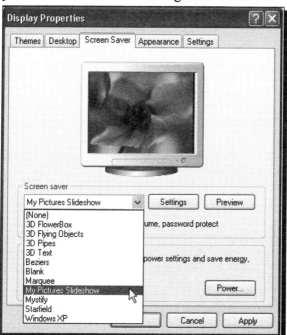

Fig. 4.5 The Themes Screen of the Display Properties Dialogue.

Selecting **My Pictures Slideshow** option as a screen saver allows you to rotate through the contents of the **My Pictures** folder. Left-click the **Settings** button to specify how often the picture changes, how big the picture should be, and whether to stretch small pictures, etc., as shown in Fig. 4.6, then click **OK** to return to the Display Properties dialogue box. For the new settings to take effect, click the **Apply** button.

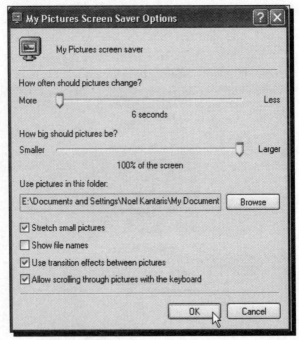

Fig. 4.6 The My Pictures Screen Saver Options.

- Click the Appearance tab to select a different look for your windows and buttons, apply a different colour scheme and select a different font size - best left as it is.

Controlling Printers

When you upgraded to Windows XP your printers should have been installed automatically. If not, you would have been stepped through the Add Printer Wizard.

Nearly 1,000 different printers are supported by Windows XP so, hopefully, you shouldn't have too much trouble getting yours to work. The printer and printing functions are included in a single Printers and Faxes folder. To open it, either double-click its icon (shown to the left), in the **Control Panel** or click its entry in the *start* cascade menu.

Printers and Faxes

Our Printers and Faxes folder, shown in Fig. 4.7, has several printers available for use. Items in the list of **Printer Tasks** provide a way of adding new printers, configuring existing ones, and managing print jobs.

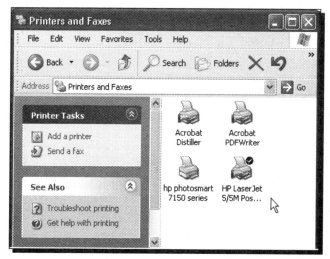

Fig. 4.7 The Printers Folder.

Windows XP, supports the following printer set-up methods:

- Plug and Play printers are automatically detected at installation time, or during the boot-up process. You will be prompted for the necessary driver files if they are not already in the Windows directory, these should be supplied with a new Plug-and-Play printer.

- Point and Print printing enables you to quickly connect to, and use, printers shared on some other networked PCs.

- For other situations, the Add Printer Wizard steps you through the printer installation process, whether the new printer is connected to your PC, or on a network.

Installing an additional printer (not connected to your system, but available to you, say, at work) allows you to use the additional fonts available to that printer. Documents prepared with such a selected printer, can then be printed to file on a 3½" floppy disc (if they are less than 1.44 MB in size) or a recordable compact disc (CD-R), and later printed out on the selected printer at the other location.

To install such an additional printer, click the **Add a printer** entry in the **Printer Tasks** list of the Printers and Faxes window, as shown here. This opens the Add Printer Wizard, which makes the installation process very easy indeed by following the on-screen instructions.

Configuring your Printer

To configure your printer, left-click the Printers and Faxes icon in the *start* cascade menu, select the printer you want to configure, and click the **Set printer properties** option in the **Printer Tasks** list pointed to in Fig. 4.8 below. This opens the Properties dialogue box for the selected printer.

Fig. 4.8 The Printer and Faxes Window.

From the displayed tabbed dialogue box you can control all the printer's parameters, such as the printer port (or network path), paper and graphics options, built-in fonts, and other device options specific to the printer model. All these settings are fairly self explanatory and as they depend on your printer type, we will leave them to you.

A newly installed printer is automatically set as the default printer, indicated by a tick against it. To change this, select a printer connected to your PC, right-click it, and choose the **Set as Default Printer** option on the displayed shortcut menu.

Once you have installed and configured your printers in Windows they are then available for all your application programs to use. The correct printer is selected usually in one of the application's **File** menu options.

Managing Print Jobs

If you want to find out what exactly is happening while a document or documents are being sent to your printer, double-click the printer icon on the right end of the Task bar, to open its window.

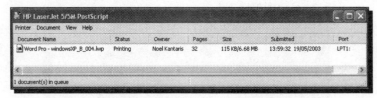

Fig. 4.9 The Print Queue Window.

As shown in Fig. 4.9, this displays detailed information about the contents of any work actually being printed, or of print jobs that are waiting in the queue. This includes the name of the document, its status and 'owner', when it was added to the print queue, the printing progress and when printing was started.

You can control the printing operation from the **Printer** and **Document** menu options of the Print Queue window, from the object menu, or from the **Printer Tasks** list. Selecting **Printer, Pause Printing** will stop the operation until you make the same selection again; it is a toggle menu option. The **Cancel All Documents** option will remove all, or selected, print jobs from the print queue. However, be patient as the deleting process takes its time.

Installing a Fax Printer

Windows XP includes its own Fax printer driver. To install it, open the **Printers and Faxes** folder, shown in Fig. 4.8, and click the **Install a local fax printer** entry in the Printer Tasks box as shown in Fig. 4.10 below.

Fig. 4.10 The Printers and Faxes Dialogue box.

This starts the Install Fax Wizard which might ask you to insert the Windows XP distribution CD in the CD-ROM drive so that required files can be copied. Once that is done, a Fax printer is installed.

All the printers installed on your system are available to you from within any of the word processing or other applications you might have on your computer so that you can either print a document to your local printer, to a shared printer (if you are connected to a network) or the Fax printer (if you are connected to a phone line). To send and receive Faxes all you need is a fax device, such as a Fax modem - it must support Fax capabilities, not just data standards.

Exercise

For the following exercise, we suggest you use a friend you can rely on to respond to your first Fax, so that you can find out if your system is set up and functioning correctly. It might be a good idea to phone first!

1. To begin the process, write a short message using your favourite word processor, then do the following:

   • Select your word processor's **File**, **Print** menu command and on the displayed Print dialogue box choose to print to **Fax**, as shown in Fig. 4.11.

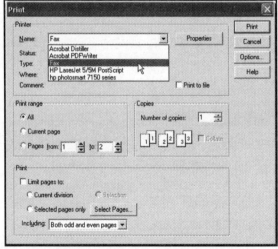

Fig. 4.11 Selecting the Fax Printer.

   • Press **Print** to start the **Send Fax** Wizard which displays its welcome screen. As usual, you progress through the various Wizard screens by clicking the **Next** button. On the second Wizard screen you are asked to insert the name of the recipient (there can be more than one) and their Fax number, as shown in Fig. 4.12 on the next page.

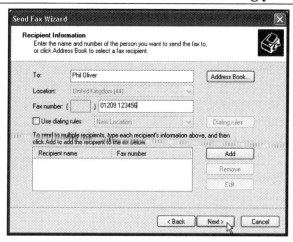

Fig. 4.12 The Second Send Fax Wizard Screen.

- Alternatively, you could click the **Address Book** button, select the Main Identity's Contacts from the drop-down list, then choose the person you want to send a Fax to, as shown in Fig. 4.13. The Address book will be discussed in the next section.

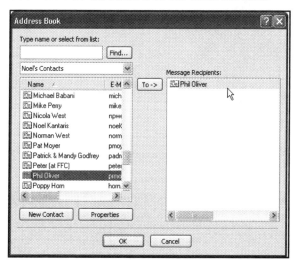

Fig. 4.13 Selecting a Recipient from the Address Book.

- Pressing the **OK** button, displays the fourth Wizard screen, in which you can add more recipients, or remove a selected one. In the fifth Wizard screen you can select one cover page template from a drop-down list, type a few words in the **Subject line** box, and your main message in the **Note** box. Pressing the **Next** button, displays the sixth Wizard screen in which you can select to send the Fax now or later when it might be cheaper. All these are self-explanatory and we will leave it to you to explore.

- Clicking the **Next** button, completes the Send Fax Wizard by displaying the summary screen, as shown in Fig. 4.14 below.

Fig. 4.14 The Last Send Fax Wizard Screen.

- Finally, click the **Finish** button to activate the Fax Monitor which rings the specified number, and sends the Fax.

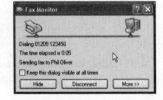

The Fax Console

To see the Fax Console, click *start*, **All Programs**, **Accessories**, **Communications**, **Fax**, then select **Fax Console** from the displayed options. The **Fax Console**, shown in Fig. 4.15, displays incoming and outgoing Faxes and allows you to view and manage your Faxes.

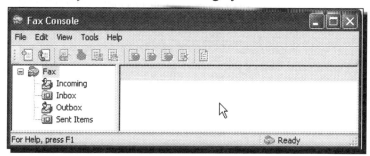

Fig. 4.15 The Address Book Screen.

The **File** menu options allow you to send a Fax (it starts the Send Fax Wizard) - you can use the information held in your Address Book, and specify multiple recipients for the one Fax. You can also receive a Fax now, view, print, save and mail a copy of it to someone else. While a Fax is being sent, you can pause or resume its transmission, restart or delete it. Incoming Faxes are intercepted by your PC and can be read on screen.

The **Edit** menu options allow you to select Faxes in various ways for further operations.

The **View** menu options allow you to configure what you see and how you see it on the **Fax Console**.

The **Tools** menu options allow you to enter sender information, create, open, copy or delete personal cover pages, display the Fax printer's status, start the Fax Configuration Wizard, or display the Fax Properties.

The Address Book

The Address Book can be used not only with the Fax utility, but also with the E-mail utility (to be discussed in the next chapter). Although Fax numbers are straight-forward to deal with, e-mail addresses are often quite complicated and not at all easy to remember. Windows provides an Address Book in which Fax numbers, telephone numbers, and e-mail addresses can be gathered together and used by its various communication utilities.

To access the Address Book, use the *start*, **All Programs**, **Accessories** menu command, and select the **Address Book** option. In Fig. 4.16 below, we show part of an example.

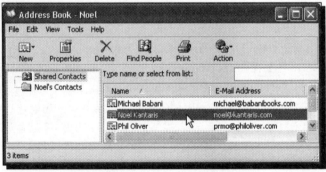

Fig. 4.16 The Address Book Screen.

Once in the Address Book, you can manually add a person's details, Fax number and e-mail address, in the Properties box that opens when you click the New Toolbar icon and select **New Contact**, as shown here. Selecting **New Group** from this drop-down menu lets you create a grouping of e-mail addresses, you can then send a Fax or an e-mail to everyone in the group with one operation.

The **New Contact** button lets you add details for a new person to the Address Book, and the **Properties** button lets you edit an existing entry, as shown in Fig. 4.17 below.

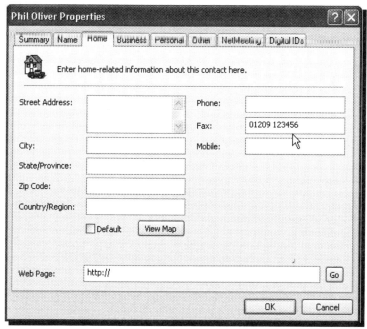

Fig. 4.17 A Recipient's Properties Screen.

The Home tab screen is used to enter the recipient's address, telephone and Fax number. You can also enter similar information for Business. Use the Name tab to enter the name, title, and e-mail address for the recipient. Transferring information about your contacts (at this stage, name, Fax number, and e-mail address) will save you a lot of time in the future. The rest of the information pertaining to an individual can be entered later as it is needed, by editing an Address Book entry. Do investigate the other tab screens by yourself.

Address Book Help

We will leave it to you to find your way round this very
comprehensive facility. Don't forget that it has its own
Help system that you can use with the **Help, Contents
and Index** menu command. An example section is shown
open in Fig. 4.18.

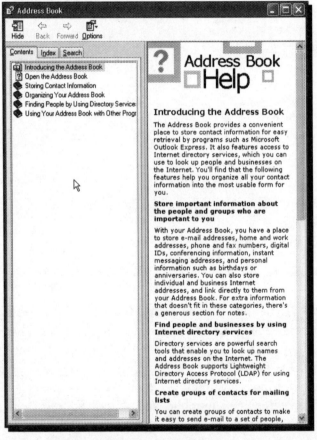

Fig. 4.18 The Address Book Help System.

Adding Hardware to your System

Windows XP automates the process of adding hardware to your system by including a set of software standards for controlling suitably designed hardware devices.

Plug-and-Play: Windows supports what are known as Plug-and-Play compatible devices. So, when you buy new hardware, make sure that it is Plug-and-Play compatible. Adding such hardware devices to your system is extremely easy, as Windows takes charge and automatically controls all its settings so that it fits in with the rest of the system.

Add New Hardware Wizard: If your new hardware is not Plug-and-Play compatible all is not lost, as there is a very powerful Wizard to help you with their installation. Fit the new hardware before you run the Wizard, as it is just possible that Windows will recognise the change and be able to carry out the configuration by itself.

If the new hardware is not recognised, start the Wizard by double-clicking the Add New Hardware icon in the **Control Panel**, shown here, and follow the instructions. The Wizard searches your system for anything new, which takes a few seconds to complete. Then, if the new hardware is not recognised, a list of the installed hardware is displayed and you are asked to specify the type of new hardware

If your new hardware has come with a CD and Windows asks you, insert it in the CD-ROM drive, as Windows might need hardware drivers which are usually supplied by the hardware manufacturer.

Adding Software to your PC

Installing Windows applications is very easy with

Windows XP. Place the CD, or the first disc, with the software on it in its drive, double-click the **Add or Remove Programs** icon in the Control Panel and click the **Add New Programs** option button on the left of the displayed

dialogue box, shown here in Fig. 4.19. The disc drives will be searched and you will be asked to confirm what you want installed.

Fig. 4.19 The Add or Remove Programs Dialogue Box.

The **Change or Remove Programs** option icon only works for programs on your system that were specially written for Windows and are listed in the dialogue box (Fig. 4.19). Using this option removes all trace of the selected program from your hard disc, although sometimes the folders are left empty on your hard drive. These can be removed manually later by using **My Computer** to find the main folder in which the software was originally installed.

Adding/Removing Windows Features

The **Add/Remove Windows Components** option icon in Fig. 4.19, allows you to install or remove specific Windows components at any time. To install or remove such features, open the dialogue box, shown in Fig. 4.20, highlight the group that contains them and click **Details**.

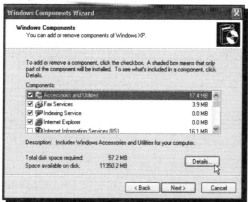

Fig. 4.20 The Windows Components Wizard.

This examines your system and lists the components of the chosen group (Fig. 4.21). Clicking the box to the left of an item name will install the selected component, while any items with their ticks removed, will be uninstalled.

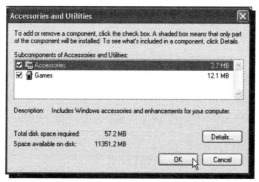

Fig. 4.21 The Accessories Dialogue Box.

You will need to have the original Windows XP CD available, and when you have made the selections you want, keep clicking **OK** to carry out the required changes. It is easy to use up too much hard disc space with Windows XP features, so keep your eye on the **Total disk space required** entry.

Checking your Regional Settings

Most Windows application programs use Windows settings to determine how they display and handle, time, date, language, numbers, and currency. It is important that you ensure your system was correctly set up during the installation process.

 Use the **Start**, **Control Panel** option, then double-click the **Regional and Language Options** icon, shown here, to open the tabbed dialogue box shown in Fig. 4.22 on the next page.

Make sure the various entries are correct. If not, change them by clicking the down arrow to the right of an entry to display a drop-down list and select the most appropriate country and language in the tabbed pages of the dialogue box.

If, in the future, you start getting '$' signs, instead of '£' signs, or commas in numbers where you would expect periods, check your regional settings and click the **Customize** button to change the way currency, time, and date display. You will have to click the **Apply** button before any changes become effective.

Fig. 4.22 The Regional Settings Properties Box.

To change the actual time and date of your computer's clock, double-click the clock displayed at the bottom right corner of the Windows screen.

* * *

In chapter 5 and 6 we discuss how to connect to the Internet and how to send and receive e-mail using Outlook Express. Chapter 5 covers the basics, while Chapter 6 delves into e-mail attachments and e-mail organisation.

5

E-mail - Outlook Express Basics

To be able to communicate electronically with the rest of the world, many users will need to connect their PC through a modem to an active phone line. This is a device that converts data so that it can be transmitted over the telephone system. Installing such a modem is quite easy with Windows XP.

Modem Properties

Before using your modem, check to ensure it is correctly

 configured. To do this, double-click the **Phone and Modem Options** icon in the **Control Panel**. Windows will open the Options window (Fig. 5.1), with its Modems tab selected. Click the **Properties** button, then select the Diagnostics tab and click the **Query Modem** button.

Fig. 5.1 Phone and Modem Options Window.

If it displays the word 'success', as shown in Fig. 5.2, your modem is working fine. If not, make sure it is connected correctly, and if an external modem that it is switched on. Obviously, unless you can get your computer to communicate with your modem, none of what follows can be achieved.

Fig. 5.2 Your Modem's Diagnostics.

Microsoft Outlook Express

Windows XP comes with the very powerful mail and news facility, Outlook Express 6, built into it, which makes it very easy for you to send and receive e-mail messages. The program should already have been added to your PC by **Setup** (an entry being placed on the **Start** menu left column. Some users might prefer to have a shortcut to Outlook Express on their desktop (right-click it and use the **Send To**, **Desktop** command, while others might prefer to have it placed in the Quick Launch area of the Task bar (drag it there). The choice is yours!

To start the program, left-click the menu option on the *start* menu, shown here, double-click its icon on the desktop, or click its icon on the Quick Launch Toolbar. Either of these actions displays the screen shown in Fig. 5.3 on the next page.

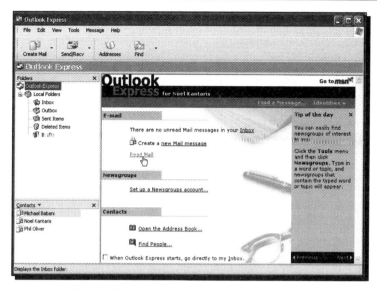

Fig. 5.3 The Outlook Express Opening Screen.

Obviously, to send and receive electronic mail over a modem, you must make an arrangement with a commercial server. There are quite a few around now, and most have Internet options. Try and find one that is free or can provide you with a reduced rate for local telephone calls, to minimise your phone bills. Once you have registered with such a service, you will be provided with all the necessary information to enter in the Internet Connection Wizard, so that you can fully exploit all the available facilities.

Connecting to your Server

To tell Outlook Express how to connect to your server's facilities, you must complete your personal e-mail connection details in the Internet Connection Wizard, which opens when you first attempt to use the Read Mail facility pointed to in Fig. 5.3.

If the Wizard does not open, or if you want to change your connection details, use the **Tools**, **Accounts** menu command, select the mail tab and click the **Add** button and select **Mail**, as shown in the composite screen dump in Fig. 5.4 below.

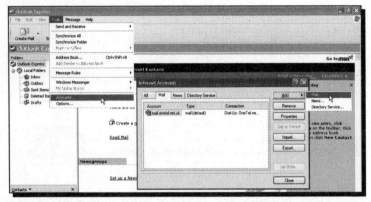

Fig. 5.4 The Internet Accounts Options Screen of Outlook Express.

In the first screen of the Wizard, type your name in the text box, as shown in Fig. 5.5 below.

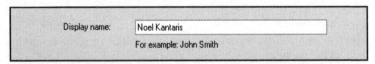

Fig. 5.5 Part of the First Internet Connection Wizard Screen.

We only show the relevant parts of the various Wizard screens so you know what is expected of you, but remember to type your own details (not what is shown) in these Wizard screens, and click the **Next** button to progress from one screen to another.

In the second screen of the Wizard, enter your e-mail address in the text box, as shown in Fig. 5.6 below.

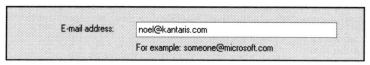

E-mail address: noel@kantaris.com

For example: someone@microsoft.com

Fig. 5.6 Part of the Second Internet Connection Wizard Screen.

If you have not organised one yet you could always sign up for free e-mail with Hotmail, which is a free browser-based e-mail service owned by Microsoft - we will discuss this in Chapter 7.

In the third Wizard screen enter your e-mail server details, as shown for us in Fig. 5.7 below. To complete some of the details here you may need to ask your Internet Service Provider (ISP), or system administrator, for help. The details shown below will obviously only work for the writer, so please don't try them!

My incoming mail server is a   POP3   ∨ server.

Incoming mail (POP3, IMAP or HTTP) server:

pop.prestel.co.uk

An SMTP server is the server that is used for your outgoing e-mail.

Outgoing mail (SMTP) server:

smtp.prestel.co.uk

Fig. 5.7 Part of the Third Internet Connection Wizard Screen.

The next Wizard screen asks for your user name and password. Both these would have been given to you by your ISP. Type these in, as shown in Fig. 5.8 on the next page.

If you select the **Remember password** option in this box, you will not have to enter these details every time you log on. **BUT** it may not be wise to do this if your PC is in a busy office - for security reasons.

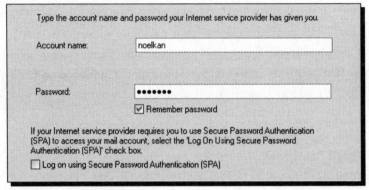

Fig. 5.8 Part of the Fourth Internet Connection Wizard Screen.

Pressing **Next**, leads to the final Wizard screen informing you of your success, which completes the procedure, so click **Finish** to return to the Internet Accounts tabbed window, with your new mail account set up as shown for us in Fig. 5.9 below.

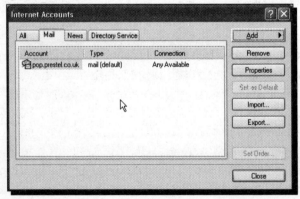

Fig. 5.9 The Internet Mail Accounts Window.

In the future, selecting the account in this box and clicking the **Properties** button will give you access to the settings sheets (to check, or change, your details).

Once your connection is established, you can click the Read Mail coloured link, or the **Inbox** entry in the Folder List to read your mail. Opening the Inbox for the first time, will probably display a message from Microsoft, like that shown in Fig. 5.10.

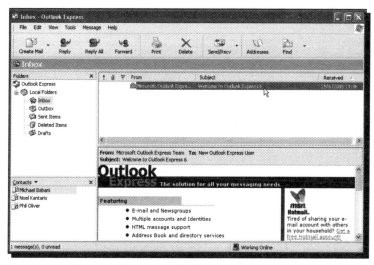

Fig. 5.10 The Inbox Outlook Express Screen.

This shows the default Outlook Express Main window layout, which consists of a Folders List to the left with a Contacts list (from the Address Book) below it, a Message List to the right and a Preview Pane below that. The list under Folders contains all the active mail folders, news servers and newsgroups. Clicking on one of these displays its contents in the Message List. Clicking on a message opens a Preview of it, while double-clicking on a message opens the message in its own window.

Receiving an E-mail

To check your mail, click the Send/Recv Toolbar icon

which will display the Dial-up Connection window shown in Fig. 5.11 below.

Clicking the **Connect** button, activates your modem and connects you to the Internet. If you have any new messages, they will be downloaded from your mailbox to your hard disc. You can then double-click on the connection image on the extreme right of the Task bar, shown here, to display your connection **Status** window (Fig. 5.12).

Fig. 5.11 The Dial-up Connection Window.

Clicking the **Disconnect** button, disconnects your PC from the Internet so you can read and process your mail at your leisure without still paying for a telephone connection.

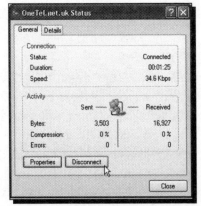

Fig. 5.12 Your Connection's Status Window.

Sending a Test E-mail Message

Before explaining in more detail the main features of Outlook Express we will step through the procedure of sending a very simple e-mail message. The best way to test out any unfamiliar e-mail features is to send a test message to your own e-mail address. This saves wasting somebody else's time, and the message can be very quickly checked to see the results. To start, click the Create Mail icon to open the New Message window, shown in Fig. 5.13 below.

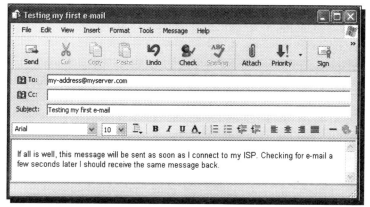

Fig. 5.13 Creating a New E-mail.

Type your own e-mail address in the **To:** field, and a title for the message in the **Subject:** field. The text in this subject field will form a header for the message when it is received, so it helps to show in a few words what the message is about. Type your message and click the Send Toolbar icon shown here.

By default, your message is stored in an Outbox folder, and pressing the Send/Recv Toolbar icon will connect to the Internet and then send it, hopefully straight into your mailbox.

When Outlook Express next checks for mail, it will find the message and download it into the Inbox folder, for you to read.

The Main Outlook Express Window

After the initial opening window, Outlook Express uses three other main windows, which we will refer to as: the Main window which opens next; the Read Message window for reading your mail; and the New Message window, to compose your outgoing mail messages.

The Main window consists of a Toolbar, a menu, and five panes with the default display shown in our example in Fig. 5.10. You can choose different pane layouts, and customise the Toolbar, with the **View**, **Layout** menu command, but we will let you try these for yourself.

The Folders List

The folders pane contains a list of your mail folders, your news servers and any newsgroups you have subscribed to. There are always at least five mail folders, as shown in Fig. 5.14 on the next page. You can add your own with the **File**, **Folder**, **New** menu command from the Main window. You can delete added folders with the **File**, **Folder**, **Delete** command. These operations can also be carried out after right-clicking a folder in the list. You can drag messages from the Message list and drop them into any of the folders, to 'store' them there.

Note the icons shown below, any new folders you add will have the same icon as that of the first added folder.

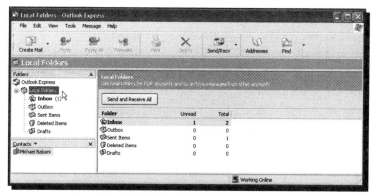

Fig. 5.14 The Local Folders Pane.

The Contacts Pane

This pane simply lists the contacts held in your Address Book. Double-clicking on an entry in this list opens a New Message window with the message already addressed to that person.

The Message List

When you select a folder, by clicking it in the Folders list, the Message list shows the contents of that folder. Brief details of each message are displayed on one line, as shown in Fig. 5.15.

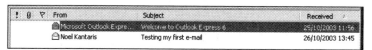

Fig. 5.15 Received Messages in Ascending Date Order.

The first column shows the message priority, if any, the second whether the message has an attachment, and the third whether the message has been 'flagged'. All of these are indicated by icons on the message line. The 'From' column shows the message status icon (see Fig. 5.17) and the name of the sender, 'Subject' shows the title of each mail message, and 'Received' shows the date it reached you. You can control what columns display in this pane with the **View**, **Columns** menu command.

To sort a list of messages, you can click the mouse pointer in the title of the column you want the list sorted on, clicking it again will sort it in reverse order. The sorted column is shown with a triangle mark, as shown in Fig. 5.16 below.

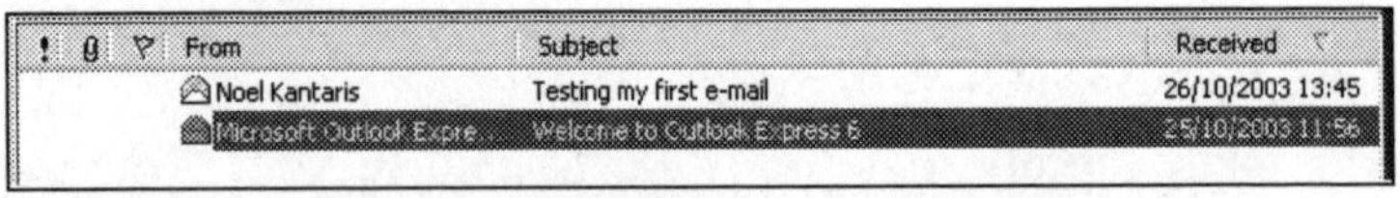

!	0	♡	From	Subject	Received ▽
			📨 Noel Kantaris	Testing my first e-mail	26/10/2003 13:45
			Microsoft Outlook Expre...	Welcome to Outlook Express 6	25/10/2003 11:56

Fig. 5.16 Received Messages in Descending Date Order.

This shows the received messages sorted by date, with the most recently received message appearing at the top. This is our preferred method of display.

The Preview Pane

When you select a message in the Message list, by clicking it once, it is displayed in the Preview pane, which takes up the rest of the window. This lets you read the first few lines to see if the message is worth bothering with. If so, double-clicking the header, in the Message list, will open the message in the Read Message window, as shown later in the chapter.

You could use the Preview pane to read all your mail, especially if your messages are all on the short side, but it is easier to process them from the Read Message window.

Message Status Icons

This icon	Indicates this
🌢	The message has one or more files attached.
❗	The message has been marked high priority by the sender.
↓	The message has been marked low priority by the sender.
⊿	The message has been read. The message heading appears in light type.
✉	The message has not been read. The message heading appears in bold type.
🖂	The message has been replied to.
🖂	The message has been forwarded.
📝	The message is in progress in the Drafts folder.
🖂	The message is digitally signed and unopened.
🖂	The message is encrypted and unopened.
🖂	The message is digitally signed, encrypted and unopened.
🖂	The message is digitally signed and has been opened.
🖂	The message is encrypted and has been opened.
🖂	The message is digitally signed and encrypted, and has been opened.
⊞	The message has responses that are collapsed. Click the icon to show all the responses (expand the conversation).
⊟	The message and all of its responses are expanded. Click the icon to hide all the responses (collapse the conversation).
📨	The unread message header is on an IMAP server.
📨	The opened message is marked for deletion on an IMAP server.
▼	The message is flagged.
↓	The IMAP message is marked to be downloaded.
⊞↓	The IMAP message and all conversations are marked to be downloaded.
⊟↓	The individual IMAP message (without conversations) is marked to be downloaded.

Fig. 5.17. Table of Message Status Icons.

The Main Window Toolbar

Selecting any one of the local folders displays the following buttons on Outlook's Toolbar.

 Opens the New Message window for creating a new mail message, with the To: field blank.

 Opens the New Message window for replying to the current mail message, with the To: field pre-addressed to the original sender. The original Subject field is prefixed with Re:.

 Opens the New Message window for replying to the current mail message, with the To: field pre-addressed to all that received copies of the original message. The original Subject field is prefixed with Re:.

 Opens the New Message window for forwarding the current mail message. The To: field is blank. The original Subject field is prefixed with Fw:.

 Prints the selected message.

 Deletes the currently selected message and places it in the Deleted Items folder.

 Connects to the mailbox server and downloads waiting messages, which it places in the Inbox folder. Sends any messages waiting in the Outbox folder.

Opens the Address Book.

 Finds a message or an e-mail address using Find People facilities of the Address Book.

The Read Message Window

If you double-click a message in the Message list of the Main window the Read Message window is opened, as shown in Fig. 5.18 below.

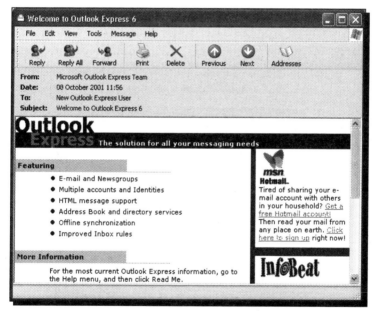

Fig. 5.18 The Read Message Window.

This is the best window to read your mail in. It has its own menu system and Toolbar, which lets you rapidly process and move between the messages in a folder.

The Read Message Toolbar

This window has its own Toolbar, but only two icons are different from those in the Main window.

Previous - Displays the previous mail message in the Read Message window.

Next - Displays the next mail message in the Read Message window.

These buttons appear depressed if there are no previous or further messages.

Signing your E-mail

You create a signature from the Main window using the **Tools**, **Options** command which opens the Options dialogue box shown in Fig. 5.19 when its Signature tab is selected and the **New** button is clicked.

Fig. 5.19 The Tools Options Window.

You could choose to **Add signatures to all outgoing messages** which is preferable, or you could leave this option blank and use the **Insert**, *Signature* command from the New Message window menu system.

The New Message Window

This is the window, shown in Fig. 5.20, that you will use to create any messages you want to send electronically from Outlook Express. It is important to understand its features, so that you can get the most out of it.

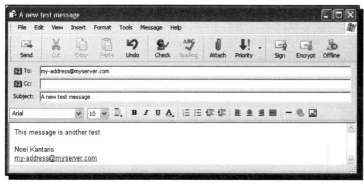

Fig. 5.20 The New Message Window.

As we saw, this window can be opened by using the **Create Mail** Toolbar icon from the Main window, as well as the **Message**, **New Message** menu command. From other windows you can also use the **Message**, **New Message** command, or the <Ctrl+N> keyboard shortcut. The newly opened window has its own menu system and Toolbar, which let you rapidly prepare (you don't need to be connected to the Internet for that), and send your new e-mail messages after connecting to the Internet.

Using Message Stationery

Another Outlook Express feature is that it lets you send your messages on pre-formatted stationery for added effect.

To access these, click the down arrow next to the **Create Mail** button in the Main window and either select from the **1** to **7** list, as shown here, or use the **Select Stationery** command to open a box with many more stationery types on offer.

Fig. 5.21 Using Stationery.

The New Message Toolbar

The icons on the New Message Toolbar window have the following functions:

Send Message - Sends message, either to the recipient, or to the Outbox folder.

Cut - Cuts selected text to the Windows clipboard.

Copy - Copies selected text to the Windows clipboard.

Paste - Pastes the contents of the Windows clipboard into the current message.

Undo - Undoes the last editing action.

Check Names - Checks that names match your entries in the address book, or are in correct e-mail address format.

Spelling - Checks the spelling of the current message before it is sent, but is only available if you have Word, Excel, or PowerPoint.

Attach File - Opens the Insert Attachment window for you to select a file to be attached to the current message.

Set Priority - Sets the message priority as high or low, to indicate its importance to the recipient.

Digitally sign message - Adds a digital signature to the message to confirm to the recipient that it is from you.

Encrypt message - Encodes the message so that only the recipient can read it.

Work Offline - Closes connection to the Internet so that you can process your mail offline. The button then changes to **Work Online.**

Message Formatting

Outlook Express provides quite sophisticated formatting options for an e-mail editor from both the **Format** menu and Toolbar. These only work if you prepare the message in HTML format, as used in Web documents. You can set this to be your default mail sending format using the Send tab in the **Tools, Options** box.

Fig. 5.22 The Format Sub-menu.

To use the format for the current message only, select **Rich Text (HTML)** from the **Format** menu, as we have done here. If **Plain Text** is selected, the black dot will be placed against this option on the menu, and the formatting features will not then be available.

The Format Toolbar shown in Fig. 5.23 below is added to the New Message window when you are in HTML mode and all the **Format** menu options are then made active.

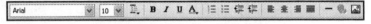

Fig. 5.23 The Format Toolbar.

As all the formatting features are self-explanatory, we will not delve into them here - most of these are quite well demonstrated in Microsoft's opening message to you. You should be able to prepare some very easily readable e-mail messages with these features, but remember that not everyone will be able to read the work in the way that you spent hours creating. Only e-mail programs that support MIME (Multipurpose Internet Mail Extensions) can read HTML formatting. When your recipient's e-mail program does not read HTML, and many people choose not to, the message appears as plain text with an HTML file attached.

Note: At the risk of being called boring we think it is usually better to stick to plain text without the selection of any message stationery; not only can everyone read it, but it is much quicker to transmit and deal with.

Replying to a Message

When you receive an e-mail message that you want to reply to, Outlook Express makes it very easy to do. The reply address and the new message subject fields are both added automatically for you. Also, by default, the original message is quoted in the reply window for you to edit as required.

With the message you want to reply to still open, click the Reply to Sender Toolbar icon to open the New Message window and the message you are replying to will, by default, be placed under the insertion point.

With long messages, you should not leave all of the original text in your reply. This can be bad practice, which rapidly makes new messages very large and time consuming to download. You should usually edit the quoted text, so that it is obvious what you are referring to. A few lines may be enough.

Removing Deleted Messages

Whenever you delete a message it is actually moved to the Deleted Items folder. If ignored, this folder gets bigger and bigger over time, so you need to check it frequently and manually re-delete messages you are sure you will not need again.

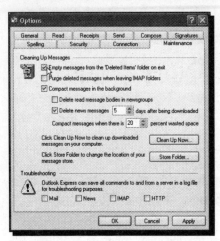

Fig. 5.24 Cleaning up Messages.

If you are confident that you will not need this safety net, you can opt to **Empty messages from the 'Deleted Items' folder on exit** in Maintenance tab settings of the **Tools, Options** box, opened from the Main window, as shown in Fig. 5.24.

* * *

In the next chapter we discuss how to send a picture or a word processed document as an attachment to an e-mail, how to organise your e-mail folders and how to print an e-mail.

6

E-mail - Some Other Features

Using E-mail Attachments

If you want to include an attachment to your main e-mail message, you simply click the **Attach** Toolbar button in the New Message window, as shown in Fig. 6.1 below.

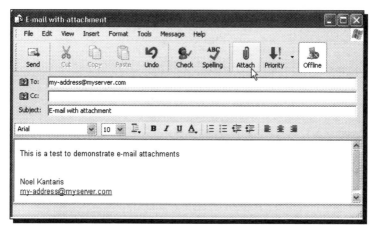

Fig. 6.1 Adding an Attachment to an E-mail.

This opens the Insert Attachment dialogue box, shown in Fig. 6.2 on the next page, for you to select the file, or files, you want to go with your message.

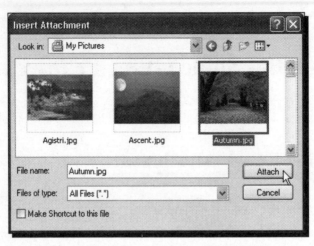

Fig. 6.2 The Insert Attachment Dialogue Box.

In Outlook Express the attached files are placed below the **Subject** text box. In Fig. 6.3 we show two attachments with their distinctive icons that tell the recipient what each file is; a Word (.doc) document file and a graphics (.jpg) file in this case.

Fig. 6.3 Adding an Attachment to an E-mail.

It is only polite to include in your e-mail a short description of what the attachments are, and which applications were used to create them; it will help the recipient to decipher them.

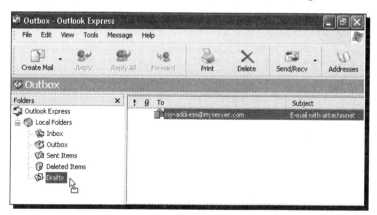

Clicking the **Send** icon on the Toolbar, puts each e-mail (with its attachments, if any) in Outlook's **Outbox** folder. Next time you click the **Send/Recv** Toolbar icon, Outlook Express connects to your ISP and sends all the e-mails stored in it.

Sending an E-mail to the Drafts Folder

If you decide that your e-mail is not complete yet and further changes are needed before sending it, click the **Outbox** folder, select its header line in the Message List and with the left mouse button depressed 'drag' it to the **Drafts** folder in the Folders List, as shown in Fig. 6.4.

Fig. 6.4 Sending an E-mail to the Drafts Folder.

To edit an e-mail waiting in the **Drafts** folder, click the folder, then double-click the e-mail to open it in its own window, edit it, and click the **Send** icon on the Toolbar.

Receiving Attachments with an E-mail

To demonstrate what happens when you receive an e-mail with attachments, we have sent the above e-mail to our ISP, then a minute or so later we received it back, as shown in Fig. 6.5 below.

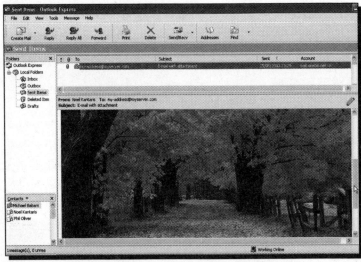

Fig. 6.5 A Received E-mail with Attachments.

Fig. 6.6 E-mail Attachments.

Note that the received e-mail shows the graphics (.jpg) file open at the bottom of the Preview pane, but there is no indication of any other attachments. To find out how many attachments were included with the received e-mail, left-click the Attach (paper clip) icon pointed to in Fig. 6.6 to display all of them.

Left-clicking a graphics (jpg) file opens it in the Photo Editor, while left-clicking the document file opens the Warning box shown in Fig. 6.7. Each attached file can be opened in situ or saved to disc by selecting **Open it** or **Save it to disk**.

Fig. 6.7 The Open Attachment Warning Window.

Organising your Messages

Probably most of the e-mail messages you get you will delete once you have dealt with them. Some however you may well need to keep for future reference. After a few weeks it can be surprising how many of these messages can accumulate. If you don't do something with them they seem to take over and slow the whole process down. That is the reason for the Folders List.

As we saw earlier you can open folders in this area, and can move and copy messages from one folder into another. You can move messages by highlighting their header line in the Message List and dragging them into another folder. The copy procedure is the same, except you must also have the <Ctrl> key depressed through the dragging procedure. You can tell that copying is taking place by the '+' on the mouse pointer.

Fig. 6.8 Moving a Message.

The System Folders

Outlook Express has five folders which it always keeps intact and will not let you delete. Some of these we have met already.

- The *Inbox* folder holds all incoming messages; you should delete or move them from this folder as soon as you have read them. Messages in the *Inbox* folder can be moved or copied into any other folder except the *Outbox* folder.

- The *Outbox* folder holds messages that have been prepared but not yet transmitted. As soon as the messages are sent they are automatically removed to the *Sent Items* folder. Messages in the *Outbox* folder can be moved or copied into any of the other folders.

- The *Sent Items* folder holds messages that have been transmitted. You can then decide whether to 'file' your copies of these messages, or whether to delete them. Messages in the *Sent Items* folder can be moved or copied into any of the other folders except the *Outbox* folder.

- The *Deleted Items* folder holds messages that have been deleted and placed in there as a safety feature. Messages in the *Deleted Items* folder can be moved or copied into any of the other folders, except the *Outbox* folder.

- The *Drafts* folder is used to hold a message you closed down without sending - the program will ask you whether to save such a message in this folder. Messages in the *Drafts* folder cannot be moved or copied into any of the other folders.

As we have seen earlier, to transmit a message held in the *Drafts* folder, double-click its header line in the Message List to open it in its own window, edit it, then click the **Send** icon on the Toolbar to transfer it into the *Outbox* folder.

To create additional folders, highlight the folder under which you want to create a sub-folder - here we have chosen to create a sub-folder under **Local Folders**. Right-clicking the selected folder and choosing the **New**

Folder option from the drop-down shortcut menu, as shown in Fig. 6.9, displays the Create Folder dialogue box shown in Fig. 6.10 below.

Fig. 6.9 Creating a New Folder.

Next, type an appropriate name for the new folder and click the **OK** button to add the newly created folder to the Local Folders list.

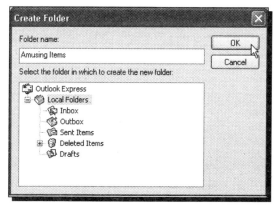

Fig. 6.10 The New Folder Dialogue Box.

Spell Checking your Messages

Just because e-mail messages are a quick way of getting in touch with friends and family, there is no reason why they should be full of spelling mistakes. Some people do not seem to read their work before clicking the 'Send' button. With Outlook Express this should be a thing of the past, as the program is linked to the spell checker that comes with other Microsoft programs. If you do not have any of these, the option will be greyed out, meaning that it is not available.

To try it out, prepare a message in the New Message window, but make an obvious spelling mistake, maybe like ours below. Pressing the Spelling Toolbar button, the **F7** function key, or using the **Tools, Spelling** menu command, reveals the drop-down sub-menu shown below in Fig. 6.11.

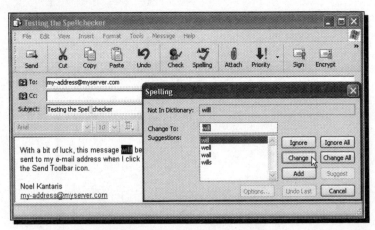

Fig. 6.11 Using the Spell Checker.

Any words not recognised by the checker will be flagged up as shown. If you are happy with the word just click one of the **Ignore** buttons, if not, you can type a correction in the **Change To:** field, or accept one of the **Suggestions:**, and then click the **Change** button. With us the **Options** button always seemed 'greyed out', but you can get some control over the spell checker on the settings sheet opened from the main Outlook Express menu with the **Tools, Options** command, and then clicking the Spelling tab.

The available options, as shown in Fig. 6.12, are self-explanatory so we will not dwell on them. If you want every message to be checked before it is sent, select the **Always check spelling before sending** option.

Fig. 6.12 The Options Spelling Dialogue Box.

You could also choose to have the Spell Checker ignore **Words with numbers**, before clicking the **Apply** button.

Connection at Start-up

While you are looking at the program settings, open the **Tools**, **Options**, Connection tabbed sheet, shown in Fig. 6.13 below.

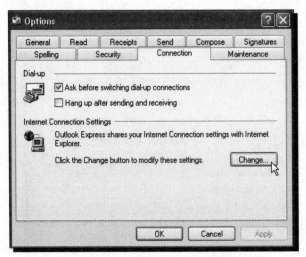

Fig. 6.13 The Options Connection Dialogue Box.

This gives you some control of what happens when you open Outlook Express, depending on your connection settings for Internet Explorer. If you have a modem connection to the Internet, it can be annoying when a program goes into dial-up mode unexpectedly. To look at these settings, click the **Change** button which displays the dialogue box in Fig. 6.14 shown on the next page.

Fig. 6.14 The Internet Properties Dialogue

Next, select the **Never dial a connection** option so that you only 'go on line' (as long as you have not chosen to **Work Offline** from the <u>F</u>ile menu option), when you click the **Send/Recv** toolbar icon shown here. If you have more than one Internet connection, the down arrow to the right of the icon lets you select which one to use.

If, on the other hand, you have a permanent Internet connection, you might like to deselect the **Never dial a connection** option.

Printing your Messages

Outlook Express lets you print e-mail messages to paper,
but it does not give you any
control over the page settings
it uses. You can, however,
alter the font size of your
printed output as it depends on
the font size you set for
viewing your messages. As
shown here, you have five
'relative'   size   options
available from the **View**, **Text**
Size menu command.

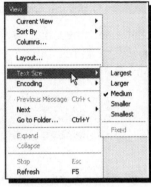

Fig. 6.15 The View Menu.

When you are ready to print a message in the Read
Message window, use the <Ctrl+P> key combination, or
the **File**, **Print** menu command, to open the Print dialogue
box shown in Fig. 6.16 with its General tab selected.

Fig. 6.16 The Print Dialogue Box.

Make sure the correct printer, **Page Range**, and **Number of copies** you want are selected, then click **Print**. You can also start the printing procedure by clicking the Print Toolbar icon shown here.

If the message has Web page links on it, there are two useful features in the Options tab of the Print dialogue box shown in Fig. 6.16. These are:

- The **Print all linked documents** option, which when checked not only prints the message, but also all the Web pages linked to it.

- The **Print table of links** option, which when checked, gives a hard copy listing of the URL addresses of all the links present in the page.

Using Message Rules

These days we seem to be in a situation of receiving e-mail messages from sources we do not want to hear from - known as junk mail. If you have this problem also, use the **Message Rules** menu option to filter your incoming messages. Unwanted ones can be placed in your **Deleted Items** folder straight away. It can also be useful for sorting incoming messages and automatically routing them to their correct folders.

To open this feature, which is shown in Fig. 6.17 on the next page, use the **Tools, Message Rules, Mail** menu command and select the criteria you want your incoming messages to be processed by.

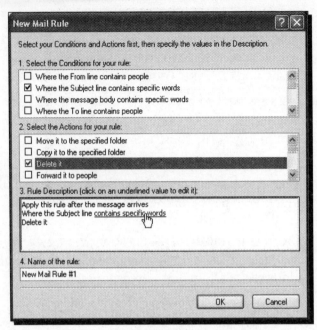

Fig. 6.17 Creating Message Rules, Box 1.

In the first box, shown in Fig. 6.17 above, you select the conditions for the new rule. In box 2 you control what actions are taken, and the new rule itself is automatically 'built' for you in box 3. If you use this feature much you will probably want to name each of your rules in box 4.

In Fig. 6.18 on the next page, we have set to intercept and delete messages which contain certain words in their Subject Lines. To complete the rule we clicked on the 'contains specific words' link and filled in the following dialogue box, clicking the **Add** button after each phrase.

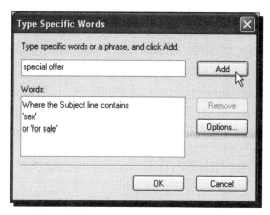

Fig. 6.18 Entering Words to Act Upon.

When finished clicking on **OK** twice opens the Message
Rules dialogue box shown in Fig. 6.19 below.

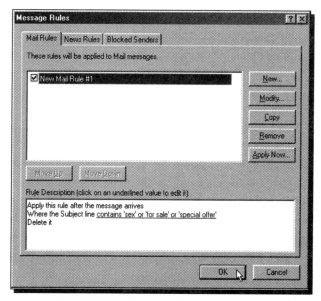

Fig. 6.19 The Message Rules Box.

In this box you can control your rules. You can set multiple rules for incoming messages and control the sort priority for the list. The higher up a multiple list a condition is the higher will be its priority.

If an incoming message matches more than one rule, then it is sorted according to the first rule it matches in your list.

The Blocked Senders List

With Outlook Express there is a very easy way to prevent messages from a problem source ever disturbing your peace again. When you first receive a problem message, select it in the Messages List and action the **Message**, **Block Sender** menu command, as we did in the example in Fig. 6.20 below.

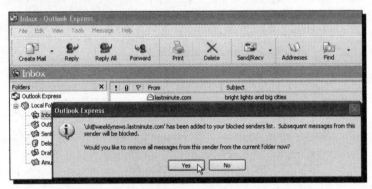

Fig. 6.20 Blocking Messages from a Single Source.

This can be a very powerful tool, but be careful how you use it. If you are not, you may block messages that you really would rather have received!

The **Message, Create Rule from Message** menu command is a quick way to start the New Rule process, as the details of the currently selected message are automatically placed in the New Mail Rule box for you.

People that send mass junk mailings often buy lists of e-mail addresses and once you are on a list you can be sure that your mailbox will never be empty again! With these tools at your disposal you should only ever receive 'junk mail' once from any particular source.

The Address Book in Outlook Express

As we have seen in Chapter 4, the Address Book is a useful utility for keeping information about your contacts. The same Address book is used by Outlook Express to refer to the same contacts and their e-mail addresses which are often quite complicated and not at all easy to remember. The Address Book can be accessed by clicking the menu icon with the same name. In Fig. 6.21 below, we show part of an example.

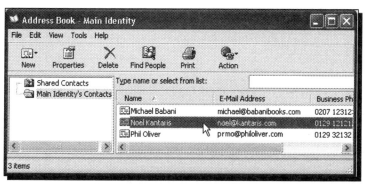

Fig. 6.21 The Address Book Screen.

Once in the Address Book, you can manually add a

person's full details and e-mail address, in the Properties box that opens when you click the New Toolbar icon and select **New Contact**, as shown here. Selecting **New Group** from this drop-down menu lets you

create a grouping of e-mail addresses, you can then send mail to everyone in the group with one operation.

To send a new message to anyone listed in your Address Book, open a New Message window and use the **Tools**, **Select Recipients** command, or click on any of the **To:** or **Cc:** icons shown here on the left.

In the Select Recipients box which is shown opened in Fig. 6.22, you can select a person's name and click either the **To:->** button to place it in the **To:** field of your message, the **Cc:->** button to place it in the **Cc:** field, or the **Bcc:->**button to place it in the **Bcc:** field.

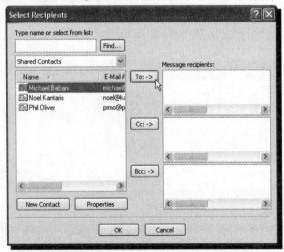

Fig. 6.22 The Select Recipients Screen.

The **Properties** button lets you edit an existing entry, and the **New Contact** button lets you add details for a new person to the Address Book, as shown in Fig. 6.23 below.

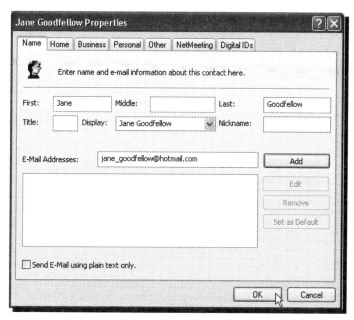

Fig. 6.23 A Recipient's Properties Screen

Fig. 6.24 Adding a Sender to the Address Book.

Clicking the **OK** button adds the new contact to your address book. To add the e-mail address of a newly received message to your Address Book, highlight the header line in the Message List and use the **Tools, Add Sender to the Address Book** menu command, as shown in Fig. 6.24.

Outlook Express Help

Outlook Express has a built-in Help system, which is accessed with the **Help**, **Contents and Index** menu command, or the **F1** function key. These open a Windows type Help window, as shown in Fig. 6.25 below.

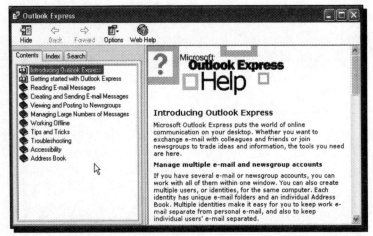

Fig. 6.25 The Outlook Express Help System.

We strongly recommend that you work your way through all the items listed in the **Contents** tabbed section. Clicking on a closed book icon will open it and display a listing of its contents. Double-clicking on a list item will then open a window with a few lines of Help information.

Another way of browsing the Help system is to click the **Index** tab and work your way through the alphabetic listing. The **Search** tab, on the other hand, opens a search facility you can use by typing your query in the **Type in the keyword to find** text field and clicking the **List Topics** button, then selecting one of the topics found and clicking **Display** to open Help information on it.

7

Using the Internet Explorer

To start the Internet Explorer, either click *start*, **All Programs**, and select **Internet Explorer** from the 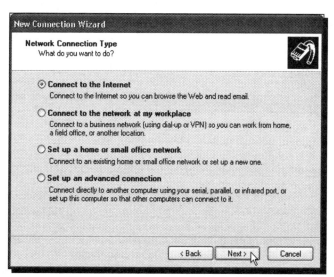cascade menu, or click its icon on the Quick Launch area of the Task bar. Clicking either of these opens the browser. The first time you do this, and if you haven't already carried out the procedure of connecting to the Internet described in Chapter 5, it will probably start the New Connection Wizard, which steps you through the process of establishing your link to the Internet.

Fig. 7.1 The New Connection Wizard.

This Wizard can make the process of setting up your Internet connection quite painless. You can open it at any time with the **Tools**, **Internet Options** menu command by clicking the **Setup** button on the **Connections** tabbed sheet. However, before starting this operation be sure to find out from your Internet Service Provider (ISP), or your system administrator, exactly what settings you will need to enter. Obviously how you complete the various options will depend on your particular system and circumstances.

After all this, and if all is well, you get your first look at the Internet Explorer browser. You may get an opening screen which may look something like that shown in Fig. 7.2., but what actually appears will depend on Microsoft, or your ISP, and will also change very often.

Fig. 7.2 A Typical First Opening Screen.

Note that when the Explorer is actually downloading data from the network, the Status Indicator on the right of the menu bar, and shown here, gives an active display and the status bar gives an indication of what is actually happening.

The default opening screen shown in Fig. 7.2 is that of **msn.co.uk**, a portal service provided by Microsoft. You can control what Web page is displayed when you start Explorer (called your home page), in the **General** settings sheet opened with the **Tools**, **Internet Options** menu command. Select **Use Current** to make any currently open page your home page, or **Use Blank** to show a clear window whenever you start up Explorer. The **Use Default** option lets you start up in **msn.co.uk** again.

Your PC Settings

Before we go any further, a few words on screen display resolutions may be useful. Your computer may well have started life set to a screen resolution of 800 x 600 pixels. It then displays a screen of 800 pixels wide and 600 pixels high on the monitor. The bigger the monitor you have, the bigger the screen resolution you can use, as everything gets smaller as the resolution goes up.

For Web browsing you want as large a resolution as you can get so that you can fit more on the screen. Web pages are almost always too large to fit on one screen. We recommend using a resolution of 800 x 600 if you have a 14" or 15" monitor, and a resolution of 1024 x 768 for 17" and larger monitors. We have already discussed how to change the screen setting in Chapter 4.

Searching the Web

There are many millions of Web pages to look at on the Web, so where do we start? You may have started already from the opening page, but there is one UK institution that we all know, and don't particularly love; 'DVLA' the Driver and Vehicle Licensing Agency. There is a lot of information on their Web site, so let's take a quick look.

Start Explorer, if it is not already going, log onto the Internet, and click the **Search** button, shown here, which is on the button bar known as the Toolbar. This

opens the Search panel on the left of the Explorer window, which should be similar to the one shown in Fig. 7.3. Next, type 'DVLA' in the text box, and click the **Search** button to 'Start Searching' the Web.

In our case, this displayed several links to pages on the DVLA site, as shown on the left panel in Fig. 7.4 on the next page.

Fig. 7.3 The Search Bar.

Explorer uses various search engines so your search may not use *msn Search*, but another one. The *msn Search* utility is just one of many search 'engines' available for finding your way round the Web. Hopefully the results will be similar.

Clicking the 'DVLA - Rates of Vehicle Excise Duty' link displays the right panel in Fig. 7.4, and from there you can choose other links that might be of interest to you.

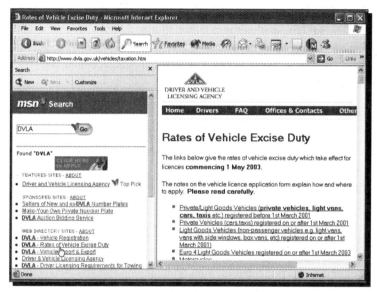

Fig. 7.4 Using the Search Bar.

The first link 'Private/Light Goods Vehicles registered before 1st March 2001' looks interesting, so click it to display the page holding the relevant information. In Fig. 7.5 the result is displayed with the 'Search' panel closed (click the **X** button), so as to maximise what can be seen on the screen. In this case we found that the engine capacity threshold for the lower taxation is 1549 cc. This is 50 cc more than we thought the figure was before carrying out this search, and the good news is that you can claim a rebate if your car meets the regulations!

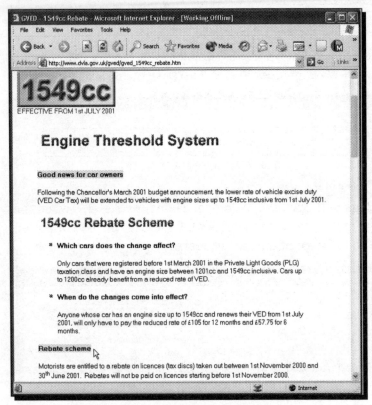

Fig. 7.5 Following Links Between Web Pages.

Other links will take you to different parts of the Web site and if you want information on renewing your licence, this is a very useful site indeed. You can even download different types of forms, such as licence renewal forms, vehicle registration forms, etc. That's the beauty of the Internet, once you find your way around you can get almost any up-to-date information you need without moving from your desk.

The Address Bar

If we had known the URL address of the site we wanted, **www.dvla.gov.uk** in our case, we could have typed it straight into the Explorer **Address** bar, as shown below.

Fig. 7.6 Using the Address Bar.

This will open the Web page shown in Fig. 7.7 when the <Enter> key on the keyboard is pressed, or the **Go** button (on the right of the bar) is clicked.

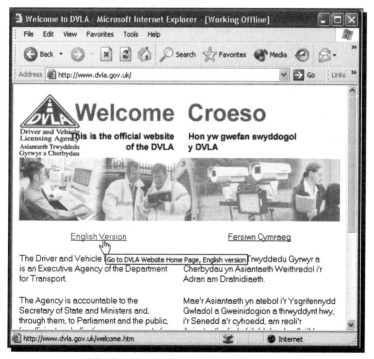

Fig. 7.7 The Welcome Page of DVLA.

The **Address** bar is the main way of opening new Web pages. If you are not connected to the Internet when you click the **Go** button, the program will start the connection procedure. A pull-down menu, opened by clicking the down-arrow at the right of the field, lets you choose from the most recent locations you have typed here, which can save both effort and errors.

Again try moving the mouse pointer around the screen. When it passes over some of the screen items it changes to a hand, as shown in Fig. 7.7. What that means is that each of these underlined text areas (or could be graphics) is actually a link to another Web page. The status bar, at the bottom of the screen, shows the URL address of the link pointed to, and the banner that opens next to the pointer describes the function of the link. Clicking any of these links on the page will open another page, which may well contain more links. We will leave it to you to explore these sites further. You may find some interesting information.

The Standard Toolbar

As we have discussed earlier in this book, Windows applications are now fully equipped with a Toolbar option, and Internet Explorer is no exception. It contains a series of buttons that you can click with your mouse pointer to quickly carry out a program function.

Fig. 7.8 The Default Standard Toolbar.

Most of the buttons are pretty self-explanatory and have the following functions:

Button	*Function*
Back	Displays the previous page viewed, or selects from the drop-down history list.
Forward	Displays the next page on the history list.
Stop	Halts any on-line transfer of page data.
Refresh	Brings a fresh copy of the current Web page to the viewer.
Home	Displays your specified home page, with a Microsoft page as the default.
Search	Opens the Search bar with access to Microsoft selected search facilities.
Favorites	Opens the Favorites bar with access to your saved favourite sites, or bookmarks.
Media	Opens the Media bar which can locate and control the playing of music and videos.
History	Opens the History bar and displays a hierarchical list of the Web pages you have previously viewed. You can browse through these again in Offline mode.
Mail	Gives quick access to your e-mail and Newsgroup facilities.
Print	Prints the open Web page, or frame, using the current print settings.

You can reach additional Standard Toolbar options by clicking the button shown here and located on the extreme right of the Standard Toolbar. One of these has the following function:

Messenger Gives you access to Chat Rooms, or starts a Wizard for you to join the Windows **.net** Messenger Service.

If the Toolbar is not showing when a window is opened, you simply open the **View** menu, select the **Toolbars** option and choose what features you want to show. This places a tick '√' character on the selected options. Selecting them again, will toggle the options off.

Favorites

Using Favorites (their spelling, not ours) which are a kind of Bookmarks, is an easy way to access the Web pages that you need to visit on a regular basis. It is much easier

to select a page URL address from a sorted list, than to look it up and manually type it into the Address field. With Internet Explorer, a Favorite is simply a Windows shortcut to a Web page.

When you first use Internet Explorer there may already be some Favorites available for you to use. Later, as your list of regular sites grows, your Favorites menu structure will grow too.

Fig. 7.9 The Favorites List.

With Explorer 6 there are two ways of accessing your list of Favorites. From the menu bar, as shown previously, and by clicking the **Favorites** Toolbar button shown here. The latter method opens the Favorites list into an Explorer bar on the left of the Explorer window, as shown in Fig. 7.10 below. This bar remains open until it is replaced by another Explorer Task bar, or either the **Favorites** button or the **X** button on the top right of the Favorites bar are clicked.

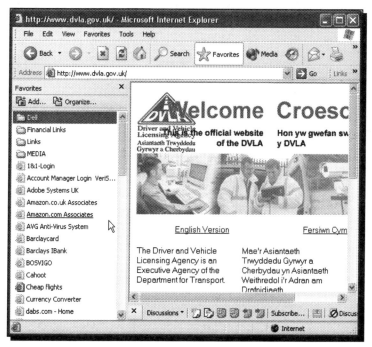

Fig. 7.10 The Favorites Bar Open.

Adding a Favorite

There are several ways to add a Favorite to the menu. When you are viewing a Web page that you want to visit again, the easiest method is to right-click on the page and select **Add to Favorites** from the object menu, as shown in Fig. 7.11.

You can also use the **Favorites**, **Add to Favorites** menu command or, if the Favorites bar is open, click its **Add** button shown in Fig. 7.10. All these methods start the same procedure by opening the Add Favorite dialogue box shown open in Fig. 7.12.

Fig. 7.11 Using the
Object Menu.

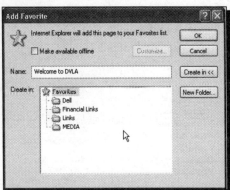

Fig. 7.12 The Add Favorites Dialogue Box.

In this example we are adding the DVLA Welcome page to our Favorite list. If your Add Favorite dialogue box does not show the list of folders, just click the **Create in** button which then opens the lower part of the box, for you to select a folder to receive the new Favorite. Clicking the **OK** button then completes the process.

History Files

Explorer stores all the Web pages and files you view on your hard disc, and places temporary pointers to them in a folder. To return to these in the future, first use the **File**, **Work Offline** command and then click the **History** icon on the Toolbar, shown here, which opens the History Explorer bar, as shown in Figure 7.13 below.

Fig. 7.13 Using the History Bar.

In this vertical bar, you can scroll offline through the sites you have recently visited. Moving the pointer over the entries will open a banner giving details of the dates, or file locations involved. Clicking on a blue 'date' icon opens a list of the sites visited. Clicking on a site will open a list of the pages you accessed there, and selecting one of these will open it so you can read it offline.

This is an excellent feature. If you pay for your Internet access by the minute, you needn't read Web pages when they are live, but just make sure they have completely downloaded, go offline and use the History Bar to work through them at your leisure.

Right-clicking on any list item gives you the options to **Expand** or **Collapse** the list, or to **Delete** it, as shown here. This gives you the option of editing out any pages you don't want to keep in the list.

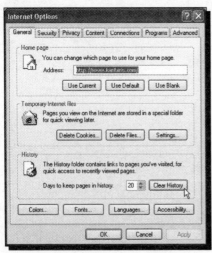

Fig. 7.14 The Internet Options.

The length of time history items are kept on your hard disc can be controlled by using the **Tools**, **Internet Options** menu command which displays the tabbed dialogue box shown in Fig. 7.14. To delete all history items click the **Clear History** button which will release the hard disc space used.

The Cache

You may have noticed that a Web page, especially one with lots of graphics, loads more quickly into Explorer if you have already recently viewed it. This is because all the pages and files you view are stored either in the History folder or in a cache folder on your hard disc, called 'Temporary Internet files'. The next time you access that page, depending on your settings, Explorer checks to see if the page has been updated before bringing it to the screen. If any change to the page has occurred, the new version is downloaded. If not, a cached copy is quickly retrieved.

As with the History files, you control the cache, from the Internet Options dialogue box. The Temporary Internet files section of the General settings tabbed sheet is shown in Fig. 7.14 on the previous page. Pressing the **Delete Files** button will clear the cache, which will very rapidly free up space on your hard disc.

Finally, in the **Internet Options** dialogue box of Fig. 7.14, you can change the Web site which is displayed when you first start **Internet Explorer**. The default Web site is that of Microsoft's **msn**. To change it to one of your choice, type its URL in the **Address** text box (or navigate to it and click the **Use Current** button), then click the **Apply** button. In this way, when you start **Internet Explorer** (or click the **Home** Toolbar button, shown here, while connected to the Internet), the Web page of your choice will be displayed, instead of Microsoft's **msn**. You can also have a blank page loaded on starting the Explorer. The choice is yours!

msn Hotmail

If you don't have a mail account with an Internet Service Provider you can always use **msn Hotmail** (owned by Microsoft), where your messages are stored on a server as Web pages. Using it you can access your e-mail from any computer with an Internet connection, anywhere in the world.

You have to be live to sign up with Hotmail, so you may have to do it from work, or a friend's PC, or a Cyber Cafe. You can't do this any more from **Outlook Express** itself, so open **Internet Explorer** and enter the following URL into the Address box:

www.hotmail.com

This opens the Hotmail home page shown in Fig. 7.15 below.

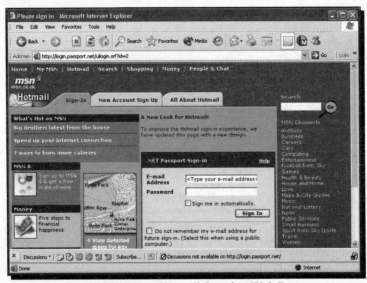

Fig. 7.15 The msn Hotmail Opening Web Page.

For a full description of Hotmail's facilities you can use the **All About Hotmail** tab near the top of the screen. Next, click the **New Accounts Sign Up** tab, which should open a registration screen similar to the one in Fig. 7.16 below.

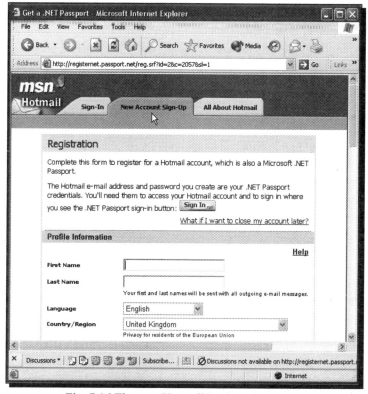

Fig. 7.16 The msn Hotmail Registration Page.

Fill in this form carefully, including the text box asking you whether you can see a displayed picture or not, and click the **I Agree** button at the bottom of the form. If you are asked to type in the characters shown in the picture box (a security measure), do so without typing any spaces.

In our case after only a few minutes we were registered and presented with the screen in Fig. 7.17.

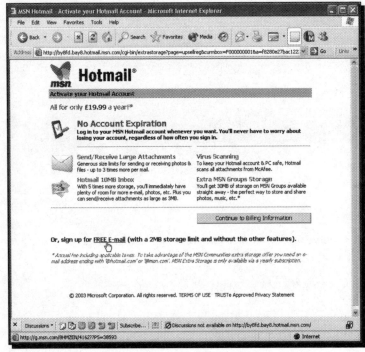

Fig. 7.17 Activating your msn Hotmail Account.

As can be seen above, you have the choice of either paying a small yearly sum to keep your chosen e-mail address for as long as you pay without any restrictions, or get a free e-mail address which has to be used often, or will be lost! The **Continue at Hotmail** button passes you through some unwelcome advertising screens and finally to the e-mail site shown in Fig. 7.18 on the next page.

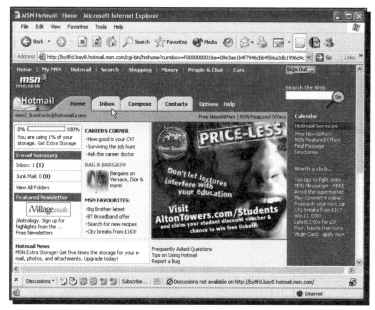

Fig. 7.18 Our Individual Hotmail Home Page.

That's as far as we will go with Hotmail. If you are interested, you can explore and learn more by using the e-mail features.

We suggest you set your Hotmail home page as one of your Favorites, or even your own home page. That way it is very easy to access it in the future. You could also use it to carry on with your Web surfing when you have checked your messages. Good luck.

Explorer Help

Internet Explorer 6 has a built-in Help system, which is accessed with the **Help, Contents and Index** menu command. This opens a Windows XP type Help window, as shown in Fig. 7.19.

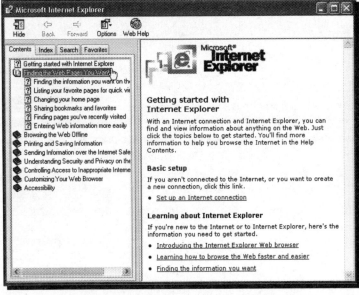

Fig. 7.19 Using Help with Internet Explorer.

Clicking on a closed book icon will open it and display a listing of its contents. Double-clicking on a list item will open a window with a few lines of Help information on the topic. We strongly recommend that you work your way through all the listed items. Another way of browsing the Help system is to click the **Index** tab and work your way through the alphabetic listing.

The **Favorites** tab opens a page that lets you store help screens that you may want to refer to again, while the **Search** tab opens a search facility you can use to find specific topics. You can also access product support from Microsoft by using the **Help, Online Support** menu command and following the available links.

If you want to know more on **Internet Explorer** or **Outlook Express**, then may we suggest you take a look at our book *Internet Explorer 6 and Outlook Express 6 explained* (BP513), also published by Bernard Babani (publishing) Ltd.

8

Accessibility, Scanners and Cameras

In this chapter we will examine how you can adjust your PC's settings for vision, hearing and mobility. We begin by using the **Start**, **Control Panel** menu command which displays the screen in Fig. 8.1 below.

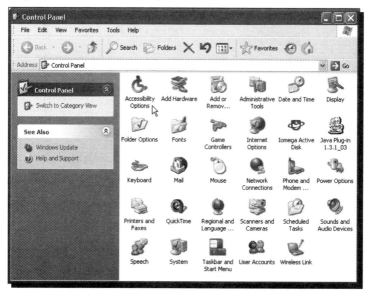

Fig. 8.1 The Control Panel Screen in Category View.

If the **Control Panel** screen displays in Category View, click the **Switch to Classical view** option to be found at the top-left panel of the screen.

Next, click the **Accessibility Options** icon to display the screen shown in Fig. 8.2 below.

Fig. 8.2 The Accessibility Options Screen.

Windows XP gives you the opportunity to make your PC more accessible to individuals who have difficulty typing or using a mouse, have slightly impaired vision, or are hard-of-hearing.

Clicking each tab in turn on this Accessibility Options dialogue box displays screens on which you can change the behaviour of the keyboard, sound, display, mouse and other general categories.

The Keyboard Options

Activating the **StickyKeys** option (Fig. 8.2), allows the user to press a modifier key such as <Ctrl>, <Alt>, <Shift>, or the <Windows Logo> and keep it active until another, but different, key is pressed. This is useful to people who have difficulty pressing two keys simultaneously.

Activating the **FilterKeys** option, instructs the keyboard to ignore brief or repeated keystrokes. The keyboard repeat rate can also be adjusted.

Activating the **ToggleKeys** option, instructs your PC to play a high-pitched sound when the <Caps Lock>, <Scroll Lock>, or <Num Lock> keys are on and low-pitched sound when they are off.

The **Settings** buttons against each of the above options allow for fine tuning of these preferences.

The Sound Options

Activating the **SoundSentry** option on the Sound tabbed sheet, shown in Fig. 8.3 on the next page, instructs your PC to flash part of its screen every time the system's built-in speaker plays a sound. Once this option is activated, you can click the down-arrow against the **Choose the visual warning** box to display a drop-down menu from which you can choose which part of the screen you want to flash.

Activating the **ShowSounds** option, instructs programs that use sound only to provide information on what they are doing at the time, to also provide visual information.

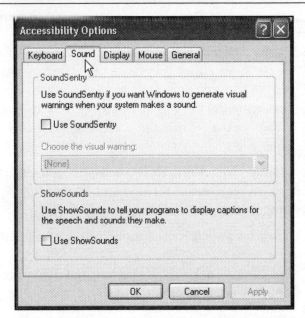

Fig. 8.3 The Sound Accessibility Options Tab Sheet.

The Display Options

Activating the **High Contrast** option on the Display tabbed sheet of the Accessibility Options screen, shown in Fig. 8.4 on the next page, instructs programs to change their colour-specific schemes to the one specified in the **Settings** sheet. Fonts are also changed whenever possible to improve legibility.

You can also change the rate at which the insertion point blinks and its width by dragging the two sliders appropriately.

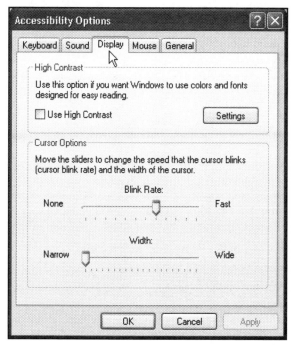

Fig. 8.4 The Display Accessibility Options Tab Sheet.

The Mouse Options

Activating the **MouseKeys** option on the Mouse tabbed sheet of the Accessibility Options screen, shown in Fig. 8.5 on the next page, allows the keys on the numeric keypad to be used to move the mouse pointer.

The shortcut key combination you need to use to activate and deactivate the numeric keypad MouseKeys is displayed   in the **Settings** sheet, where you can also change the pointer speed, and specify whether to use the MouseKeys when the Num Lock key is on or off.

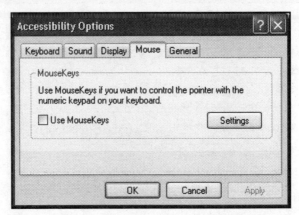

Fig. 8.5 The Mouse Accessibility Options Tab Sheet.

Once the MouseKeys option is activated, you can also use the numeric keypad to simulate mouse operations such as click, double-click, or drag. To carry out these operations, do the following:

- To click, press 5 on the numeric keypad.

- To double-click, press the plus sign (+) on the numeric keypad.

- To right-click, press the minus sign (−) on the numeric keypad, and then press 5 to click, or press the plus sign (+) to double-click.

- To click as if you were using both mouse buttons at once, press the asterisk (*) on the numeric keypad, and then press 5 to click or the plus sign (+) to double-click.

- To switch back to standard clicking, press slash (/) on the numeric keypad.

The General Options

Activating the **Automatic reset** option on the General tabbed sheet of the Accessibility Options screen, shown in Fig. 8.6 below, turns off all the accessibility features, apart from the SerialKeys option, after the specified time. The **Automatic reset** option is only used if more than one person is using the same User Account.

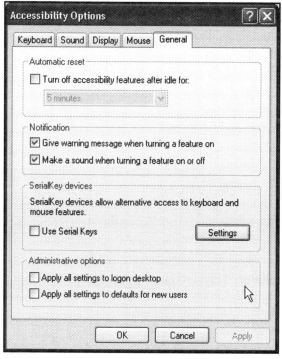

Fig. 8.6 The General Accessibility Options Tab Sheet.

Activating the **SerialKeys services** allows you to connect an alternative input device to the computer's serial port. Use the **Settings** button to display the Settings for SerialKeys screen, shown in Fig. 8.7 on the next page.

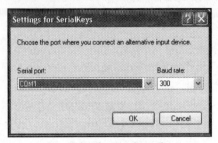

Fig. 8.7 The Settings for
SerialKeys Sheet.

Next, click the down-arrow to the right of the **Serial port** text box and choose the serial (COM) port to be used. This feature is useful for people who are not able to use the computer's standard keyboard or mouse.

For the next two sections of this chapter, we need to switch the Control Panel screen to display the Category view. To do this, click the **Switch to Category view** option to be found at the top-left part of the Control Panel screen (see Fig. 8.1). Doing this displays the screen shown in Fig. 8.8 below.

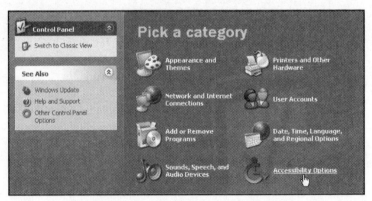

Fig. 8.8 The Control Panel in Category View.

Next, click the **Accessibility Options** entry (pointed to) under the **Pick a category** panel to display the screen shown in Fig. 8.9 on the next page.

The Microsoft Magnifier

To start the Microsoft Magnifier, click the **Magnifier** link (pointed to) under the **See Also** entry in Fig. 8.9 below.

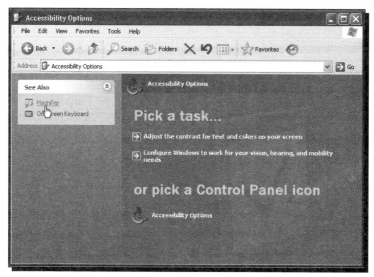

Fig. 8.9 The Magnifier link on the Accessibility Options Screen.

The displayed Magnifier screen is shown in Fig. 8.10 on the next page. The first thing to notice here is the display of the Microsoft Magnifier message, which can be prevented from displaying by clicking the **Do not show this message again** box.

However, before closing this message, note that it is magnified at the top of the screen as shown, because the mouse pointer happens to be within the actual (lower) message box. In fact, wherever you move the mouse pointer, that part of the screen is magnified in a window at the top of the screen. The magnifying window can be made bigger in the usual way.

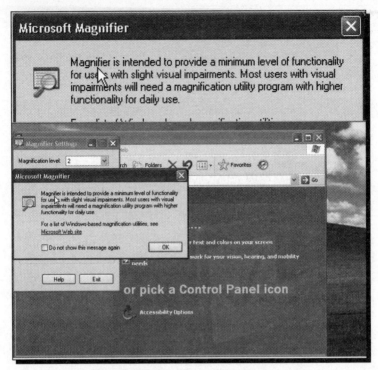

Fig. 8.10 The Magnifier Screen.

Fig. 8.11 The General
Magnifier Settings Box.

After closing the Microsoft Magnifier message box, the Magnifier Settings dialogue box becomes fully visible, as shown in Fig. 8.11. From here you can set the **Magnification level** from 1 (low) to 9 (high), and select **Tracking** and **Presentation** options. Clicking the **Exit** button removes the Magnifier facility from your screen.

Selecting **Start Minimized** under **Presentation**, minimises the Magnifier Settings box on the Task bar next time you start the Magnifier. To now exit the Magnifier, click the Magnifier Settings entry on the Task bar and remove the minimise option.

The On-Screen Keyboard

To activate the On-Screen Keyboard, click its link (pointed to) under the **See Also** entry in Fig. 8.12 below.

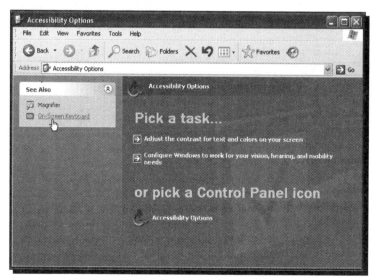

Fig. 8.12 The On-Screen Keyboard link on the
Accessibility Options Screen.

This displays the screen shown in Fig. 8.13 on the next page. The virtual keyboard allows users with mobility impairments to type data using a pointing device or joystick. The result is exactly as if you were using the actual keyboard.

Fig. 8.13 The On-Screen Virtual Keyboard.

The On-Screen Keyboard has three typing modes you can use to type data. These are:

- Clicking mode - you click the on-screen keys to type text.

- Hovering mode - you use a mouse or joystick to point to a key for a predefined period of time, and the selected character is typed automatically.

- Scanning mode - the On-Screen Keyboard continually scans the keyboard and highlights areas where you can type keyboard characters by pressing a hot key or using a switch-input device.

Fig. 8.14 The Settings Menu of the On-Screen Keyboard.

The three typing modes are selected by choosing the **Settings Typing Mode** menu command, as shown in Fig. 8.14. This opens the Typing Mode dialogue box shown in Fig. 8.15 in which you click the option you prefer and, if appropriate, the time interval before the command is actioned.

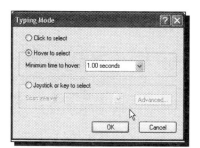

Fig. 8.15 The Typing Mode of
the On-Screen Keyboard.

Also, note that you can select from the **Settings** menu to have the virtual keyboard appear **Always on Top** of all other windows displayed on your screen, and select to **Use Click Sound** which is particularly useful if you are using the **Hover to select** option of Typing Mode.

There are several types of On-Screen Keyboards which are chosen from the **Keyboard** menu (Fig. 8.16). These are:

- The **Enhanced Keyboard** that includes the numeric keypad.

- The **Standard Keyboard** that does not include the numeric keypad.

Fig. 8.16 The Keyboard Menu of the On-Screen Keyboard.

You can also display the keyboard with the keys in the **Regular Layout**, or in a **Block Layout** (arranged in rectangular blocks). Block layout is especially useful in scanning mode. Finally, you can select to display the US standard keyboard (**101 keys**), the universal keyboard (**102 keys**), or a keyboard with additional Japanese language characters (**106 keys**).

As you can see, the Accessibility Options are many and varied, and some of these can also be used by people who have no disability whatsoever. The choice is yours!

Using a Scanner or Camera

If your scanner or digital camera are Plug-and-Play, Windows XP will detect them (if connected to your PC)

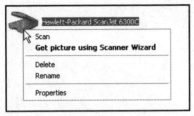

Fig. 8.17 The Scanner
Shortcut Menu.

and will start the Scanner and Camera Wizard. If your camera is not Plug-and-Play, or you are using a scanner, right-click the camera or scanner icon in **My Computer**, then click the appropriate option for that device. In Fig. 8.17 we show the shortcut menu for our scanner.

Another way of starting the Scanner and Camera Installation Wizard is to click **Start**, **Control Panel**, and then:

- If you are using the **Classic View**, double-click the **Scanners and Cameras** icon shown here.

- If you are using the **Category View**, click the **Printers and Other Hardware** link under **Pick a category**, then click the **Scanners and Cameras** link under **or pick a Control Panel icon**.

If your scanner or camera are not Plug-and-Play, follow the instructions that came with that device. It is possible, however, that you might need to get the latest driver for your device which is compatible with Windows XP or Windows 2000, by looking at your hardware manufacturer's Web site.

To start the scanning process, start the Scanner Wizard using one of the methods suggested on the previous page. After the initial Wizard page the screen shown in Fig. 8.18 is displayed.

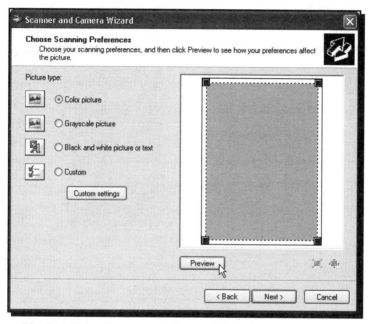

Fig. 8.18 Using Scanner and Camera Wizard to Scan a Picture.

As you can see above, there are four scanning choices; colour, grey-scale, black and white, or custom, with colour being the default. Clicking the **Preview** button activates the scanner and a preview of the picture appears on the right side of the Scanner window (Fig. 8.19).

Fig. 8.19 The Scanner Preview.

Clicking the 'enlarge preview' button pointed to in Fig. 8.19, displays the screen in Fig. 8.20. In this way you can check the result of your scanning preferences.

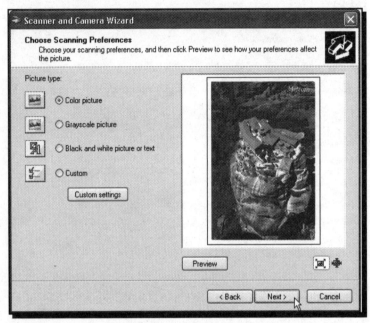

Fig. 8.20 The Enlarged Scanner Preview.

Clicking the **Next** button, displays the Wizard screen shown in Fig 8.21 on the next page, in which you can give your picture a name, select the file format and specify in which folder it should be saved. In this case, we selected the file format as Bitmap Image (**.bmp**), because in this format you get the maximum number of pixels giving best quality, which makes it ideal for printing the image in the future on photographic paper. If, however, you never intend to print this image, you might like to select the **.jpeg** file format which does not produce such large files and saves space on your hard disc.

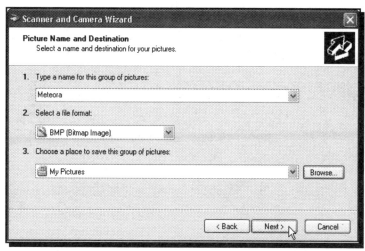

Fig. 8.21 Picture Name, File Type and Destination Screen.

Clicking the **Next** button, reactivates the scanner, re-scans and saves the picture, and displays the penultimate Wizard screen, as shown in Fig. 8.22 below.

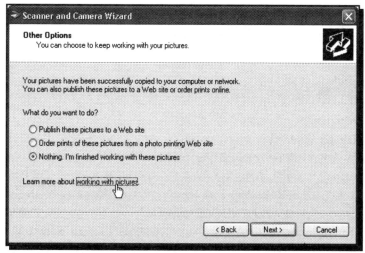

Fig. 8.22 The Penultimate Wizard Screen.

If you want to learn more about working with pictures, click the link by the same name, pointed to in Fig. 8.22, otherwise select **nothing** under the **what do you want to do?** option of the Wizard screen and click the **Next** button.

It is worth noting the size of the saved file (in this case 1,845 KB, as shown in Fig. 8.23 below) - use the **View**, **Details** menu option to see this.

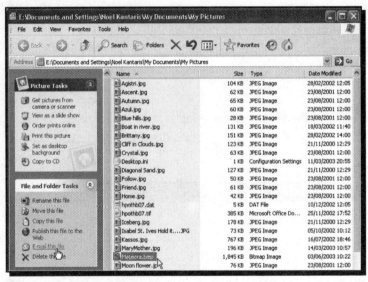

Fig. 8.23 The Penultimate Wizard Screen.

Getting pictures from your digital camera follows a similar procedure to getting pictures from a scanner. Your computer will sense the presence of your camera (if it is connected and is Plug-and-Play) and the Wizard will react appropriately. Your digital camera will, no doubt, come with its own software, as will also be the case with your scanner, so whether you use the Wizard or not, it is up to you. Nevertheless, the process is the same.

E-mailing Scanner and Camera Pictures

Should you choose to e-mail a picture obtained from your scanner or digital camera, you will be pleased to know that Windows automatically shrinks the file size for you. As we have seen, good definition pictures can be very large indeed, and sending such a file as an attachment to an e-mail can be expensive and time consuming if your connection to the Internet is via a modem.

To start the shrinking process, select the file, then click

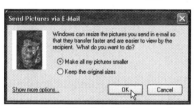

Fig. 8.24 The Send Pictures via
E-Mail dialogue box.

the **E-mail this file** option under the **File and Folder Tasks** panel, as shown in Fig. 8.23 on the previous page. This opens the dialogue box shown in Fig. 8.24.

Clicking the **OK** button attaches the picture to a new e-mail, ready for you to fill in, as shown in Fig. 8.25 on the next page.

Note that in this case the file has shrunk from 1,845 KB to a bare 35.2 KB which still looks very good on screen. However, were you to print this image, the quality on paper is passable, but not photographically excellent. That is why it is prudent to keep your pictures (particularly those from a digital camera), in their original file size and format.

Try sending one of your scanned or digital camera pictures as an attachment to an e-mail to yourself, using the method outlined above, then look at and or print the received attachment to see the result. Good luck!

Fig. 8.25 The Shrunk E-mail Attachment.

Sending Video Clips as Attachments

Some digital cameras have the facility of recording short video clips of 15-30 seconds duration in audio video interleaved (**.avi**) format - it interleaves waveform audio and digital video. These are fun to watch on your computer's Media Player, but rather large (2.5-4.5 MB) in size to send as an attachment to friends or relatives. Such files cannot be shrunk in the way scanned or digital camera pictures can, but there is a way of dealing with the problem.

To shrink such an audio video file, do the following:

- Use *start*, **All Programs**, **Accessories**, and select the **Windows Movie Maker** option from the displayed cascade menu. The program is loaded and displays on your screen as shown in Fig. 8.26.

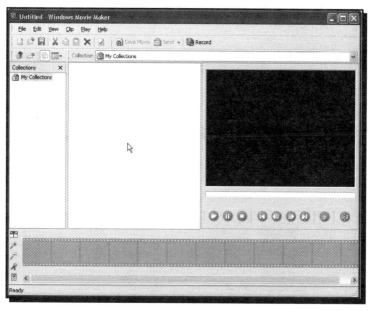

Fig. 8.26 The Movie Maker Screen.

- Next, use the **File**, **Import** command (Fig. 8.27) to open the Select File to Import dialogue box, shown in Fig. 8.28 on the next page.

- Navigate to where the video clip is to be found, click it to select it, and click the **Open** button. This imports the picture into the Movie Maker and displays the screen shown in Fig. 8.29, also on the next page.

Fig. 8.27 The File Menu of Movie Maker.

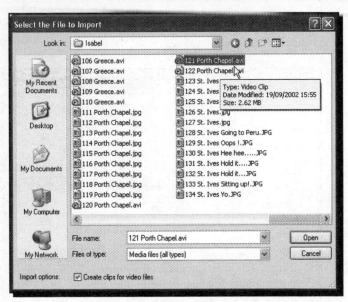

Fig. 8.28 Selecting File to Import.

Fig. 8.29 Imported File into Movie Maker.

- Next, drag the clip to the movie strip, as shown in Fig. 8.30 below.

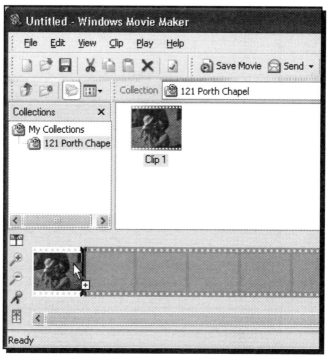

Fig. 8.30 Dragging Clip onto Movie Maker strip.

- Next, use the **File**, **Save Movie** menu option, or click the **Save Movie** icon on the Toolbar to display the Save Movie dialogue box shown in Fig. 8.31 on the next page. Under **Playback quality**, select the **High quality** setting otherwise the saved video clip might not be good enough to enjoy. Finally, give the video clip a **Title** and click the **OK** button to display the **Save As** dialogue box shown in Fig. 8.32 also on the next page.

Fig. 8.31 The Save Movie Dialogue Box.

Fig. 8.32 The Save As Dialogue Box.

- Make a note of the **Title** you gave to this video and the name under which you saved it, as these two pieces of information will be required when you attempt to send your video as an attachment. Pressing the **Save** button, creates your video and saves it under its given name in the default **My Videos** folder.

- Next, use the **File**, **Send Movie To** and select **E-mail,** or click the **Send** Toolbar icon and select **E-mail** to display a screen similar to the one shown in Fig. 8.31, where you are asked to give the **Title** of your video. Then, the Name the movie to send dialogue box is displayed asking you to enter the name of the movie file.

- Finally, the movie is created, and the **E-mail Movie** dialogue box is displayed (Fig. 8.33) in which you are asked to choose your e-mail client. In our case this is **Outlook Express**.

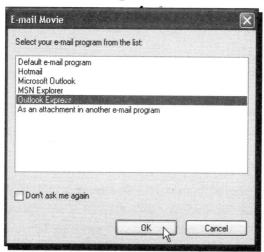

Fig. 8.33 The E-mail Movie Dialogue Box.

- Clicking the **OK** button displays the **Outlook Express** e-mail box with the movie clip ready attached, as shown in Fig. 8.34 below. All you have to do is add a short message and send it on its way.

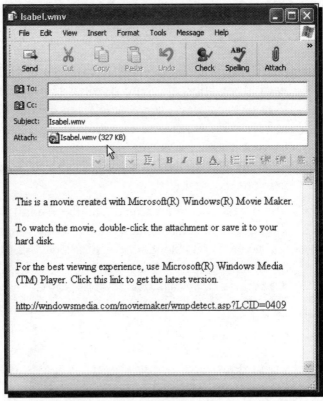

Fig. 8.34 The Outlook Express E-mail Window
with a Movie Attachment.

Note that our video clip has shrunk from 2.62 MB to 327 KB and its quality remains quite acceptable. Of course, if you don't pay telephone charges for using the Internet, then you don't have to go through this procedure.

9

Looking After your PC

Windows XP comes equipped with a full range of utilities so that you can easily maintain your PC's health. You can access all these tools by using the *start*, **All Programs**, **Accessories**, and selecting **System Tools**. This opens the menu options shown in Fig. 9.1 below.

Fig. 9.1 The System Tools Menu.

Of all the available tools, the **System Information** is the easiest to examine - it displays a number of options such as System Summary, Hardware Resources, etc. However, as each one of these is bound to be different for different PCs, we leave it to you to examine the information for your system.

Problem Prevention

Windows XP provides a threefold protection against System corruption. These are:

- System File Protection
- Automatic Update
- System Restore

These will be discussed shortly, so now all you have to look after is your data which can easily by copied to a CD as discussed earlier in the book. After all, hard discs can 'crash' and your PC could be stolen, or lost in a fire, or flood. Any of these events would cause a serious data loss, unless you had a copy of it all, and stored it safely.

System File Protection

Windows applications sometimes can, and do, overwrite important System files which, in the past, could render your system unusable. Windows XP protects such System files by automatically restoring them to their original version, if any changes have been attempted by an application program.

Automatic Update

Windows XP can update automatically any System files, if these become available, from Microsoft's Web site. All you have to do is click **Start, All Programs**, and select the **Windows Update** menu option, as shown here in Fig. 9.2.

Fig. 9.2 The Windows Update Menu Option.

After connecting to the Internet through your Internet Service Provider (ISP), you will be connected automatically to Microsoft's Web site, as shown in Fig. 9.3 below.

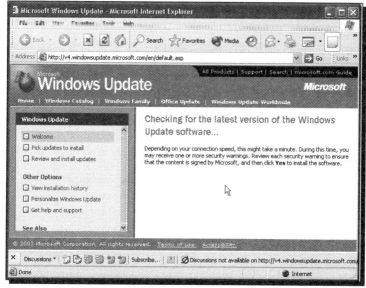

Fig. 9.3 Connecting to Microsoft's Update Home Page.

Next, click the Pick updates to install link to get an appropriate list of updates for your system. However, in order to be able to download program patches to your system, the **Windows Update** program needs to have information relating to your system configuration, as shown in Fig. 9.4. Clicking on the Scan for updates link, pointed to, causes **Update** to scan your system, which might take about a minute.

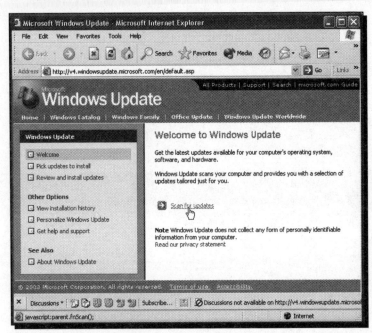

Fig. 9.4 Connecting to Microsoft's Scan for Updates Screen.

Once this is done, you can select which software to download, if any. Be careful you don't go overboard with your selection of downloads ... think of your telephone bill and the time it will take.

To give you an idea of what it is involved, we started the **Update** program for one of our computers, which had not been updated for three weeks, and the result of the process is shown in Fig. 9.5 on the next page.

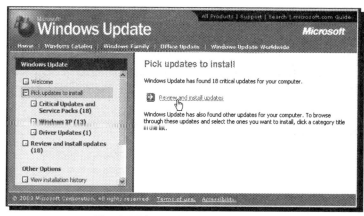

Fig. 9.5 The Updates to be Installed.

Note that there are 18 Critical Updates and Service Packs, 13 Windows XP Updates and 1 Driver Update. To see what is what before installing, click the **Review and install updates** link. This displays the screen in Fig, 9.6.

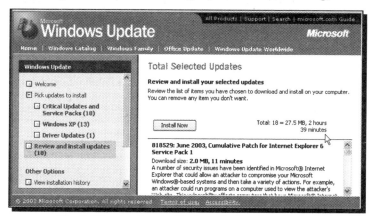

Fig. 9.6 Reviewing the Updates Before Installation.

As you can see it might be a very good idea to review these updates and select what you need before clicking the **Install Now** button. The time given for the download of 27.5 MB is very optimistic!

On successful completion of program downloads, the Windows **Setup** program installs the new patches or programs to your system automatically, after which you can either go back to browse Microsoft's site, or you can disconnect from the Internet.

New to Windows XP is the ability of the program to manage critical updates automatically as you can see on the entry in the right panel of the updates screen. We suggest you spend some time finding out a bit more about this before you commit to it.

System Restore

If things go really wrong, System Restore can be used to return your PC to the last date it was working perfectly. Every time you start to install a new program, Windows XP takes a snapshot of your system prior to starting the new installation. Alternatively, you can force Windows to take a snapshot any time you choose.

To examine the System Restore utility, use the **Start, All Programs, Accessories, System Tools** and click on its icon, shown here, which displays the screen in Fig. 9.7 on the next page. As you can see, from this screen you can select to Restore your computer to an earlier time, or create a Restore point.

To demonstrate further what happens, we chose the **Restore my computer to an earlier time** option, then clicked the **Next** button. This displays a further screen, as shown in Fig. 9.8 also on the next page.

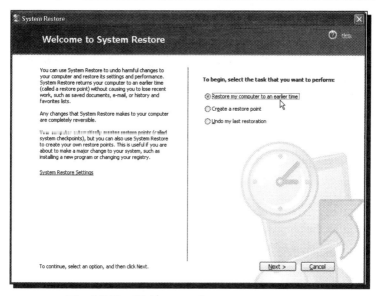

Fig. 9.7 The Welcome to System Restore Screen.

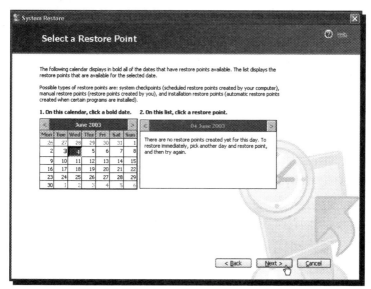

Fig. 9.8 Selecting a System Restore Point.

The dates shown in bold in the calendar are Restore points created by Windows XP. The three possible types of Restore points are:

- System Restore points created by your computer

- Manual Restore points created by you

- Restore points automatically created prior to installing certain programs.

If you select to create a Manual Restore point (you must click the **Create a restore point** option on the **Welcome to System Restore** screen), Windows XP asks you to give a description of this Restore point so that you can identify it easily at a later stage. In our example, as shown in Fig. 9.9 below, we chose to call this **After installing Windows Updates**, which together with the date given to it by the **Restore** program, gives us a pretty good clue of the circumstances surrounding its creation.

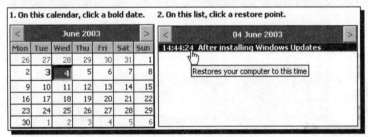

Fig. 9.9 A Manual Restore Point.

Activating the Firewall

It is a good idea to activate the Internet Connection Firewall (ICF) found in Windows XP, especially if you are using a network. A firewall is a software security system that sits between a network and the outside world and is used to set restrictions on what information is communicated from your home or small office network to and from the Internet. It protects you from uninvited outside access.

 To activate the firewall, click *start*, **Control Panel**, then double-click the **Network Connections** icon, shown here, to display the window in Fig. 9.10 below.

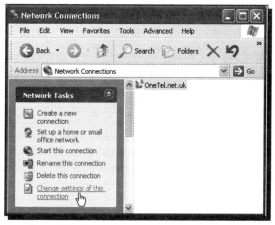

Fig. 9.10 The Network Connections Window.

Next, select the **Dial-up** connection and click the **Change settings of this connection** entry under the **Network Tasks**. In the displayed Properties dialogue box click the Advanced tab and check the **Protect my computer and network by limiting or preventing access to this computer from the Internet** box shown in Fig. 9.11.

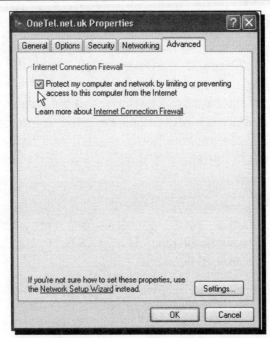

Fig. 9.11 The Advanced Properties Window.

Disk Cleanup

You can run Disk Cleanup to help you free up space on
your hard drive. The first thing that Disk Cleanup
does after activation, is to ask you to select the
drive you want to clean up, as shown in Fig. 9.12.

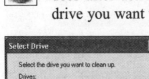

Fig. 9.12 Selecting a Drive.

It then scans the specified
drive, and then lists
temporary files, Internet
cache files, and other
program files that you can
safely delete, as shown in
Fig. 9.13 on the next page.

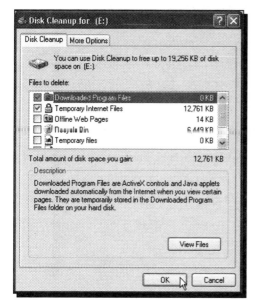

Fig. 9.13 Files Found by Cleanup.

As you can see in Fig. 9.13, we could free quite a bit of disc space by deleting the Temporary Internet Files (Web pages stored on your hard disc for quick viewing), and even more by deleting files in the Recycle Bin. The More Options tab allows you to remove some Windows components and other installed programs that you do not use any more.

Scanning a Hard Disc for Errors

Windows XP incorporates a utility that can check the integrity of your hard disc, and if it finds any errors, it can attempt to repair them. To start this utility, click My Computer then in the displayed screen right-click the drive you want to check, select **Properties** from the drop-down menu and click the **Tools** tab to display the screen in Fig. 9.14 shown on the next page.

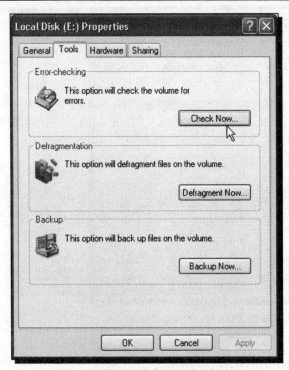

Fig. 9.14 The Disk Properties Screen.

As you can see, you have three choices; **Check Now** for disc errors, **Defragment Now**, or **Backup Now**. The last option is not available in the Windows XP Home edition. Before you can start scanning your selected drive for errors, all running programs and applications on that drive must be closed. If you start this utility while a program on that drive is running, you will be informed of the fact in a warning box.

Defragmenting your Hard Discs

The Disk Defragmenter optimises a hard disc by rearranging the data on it to eliminate unused spaces, which speeds up access to the disc by Windows operations. You don't need to exit a running application before starting the Disk Defragmenter.

Choose which drive to defragment and you can defragment it in the background while working by minimising the utility onto the Task bar. On the other hand, you can watch the process of the operation. For example, having selected a drive and clicked the **Analyze** button, you will be told whether defragmentation is needed or not. On the other hand, clicking the **Defragment** button, starts the process which is shown in Fig. 9.15 below.

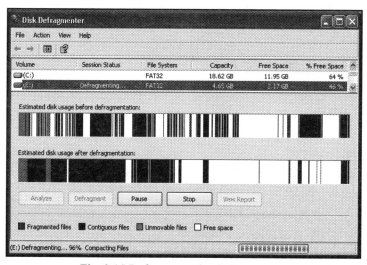

Fig. 9.15 Defragmentation in Progress.

On your screen you can see which files are fragmented (shown in red) and which files are not fragmented (shown in blue), while free space is shown in white. For large drives this process can take a long time, so do it in the background while you are working on something else, or make lots of time for it!

Scheduled Tasks

The **Scheduled Tasks** option allows you to carry out several housekeeping tasks, such as disc cleanup, or defragmenting your data, at times convenient to you. Clicking its icon, opens the window shown in Fig. 9.16 below.

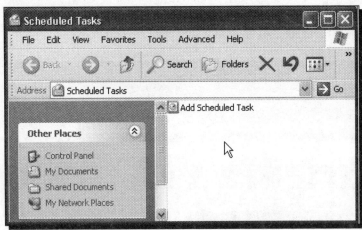

Fig. 9.16 The Scheduled Tasks Window.

Next, double-click the **Add Scheduled Task** icon to start the Wizard. Clicking **Next** on the first Wizard screen displays the second Wizard screen, shown in Fig. 9.17 on the next page.

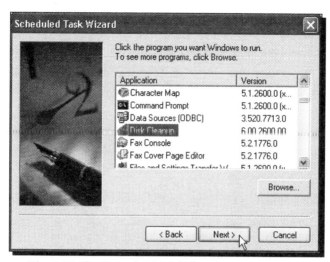

Fig. 9.17 The Second Scheduled Task Wizard Screen.

On this screen, select the task to be Scheduled then click the **Next** button to display Fig. 9.18.

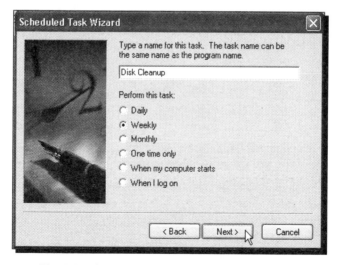

Fig. 9.18 The Third Scheduled Task Wizard Screen.

On the screen of Fig. 9.18 you are asked to specify the frequency at which you would like the selected task to be performed (we selected weekly in our example). Having done so, press the **Next** button to display the fourth Wizard screen, shown in Fig. 9.19 below.

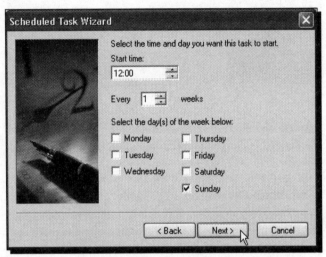

Fig. 9.19 The Fourth Scheduled Task Wizard Screen.

On this screen you are asked to specify when you want the selected task to be carried out. Obviously, your computer must be switched on in order to perform such scheduled tasks, so it's up to you to choose a convenient time. Having done so, press the **Next** button to display the fifth Wizard screen, shown in Fig. 9.20 on the next page.

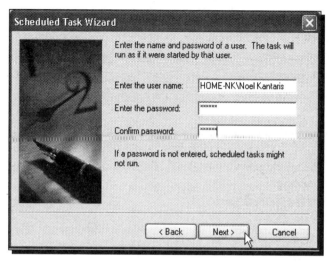

Fig. 9.20 The Fifth Scheduled Task Wizard Screen.

As you can see from the above Wizard screen, you can enter the name of a user and a password. The task is then run as if it were started by the specified user. Clicking **Next**, displays the final Wizard screen and clicking the **Finish** button, performs the selected task at its chosen time.

It is a good idea to perform such tasks regularly, but make sure that

- your computer is switched on at the selected times, and

- you are not inconvenienced by your time selection.

It is, of course assumed that your PC's clock is showing the same time as your watch, otherwise you might get some unexpected surprises!

Power Saving Management

You can automatically put your computer into hibernation or standby, provided   you log on as an administrator, and your computer is set up by the manufacturer to support these options. If your computer is connected to a network, network policy settings may prevent you from completing these tasks.

Hibernation Mode

When your computer is put into hibernation mode, everything in the computer memory is saved on your hard disc, and your computer is switched off. When you turn the computer back on, all programs and documents that were open when you turned the computer off are restored on the desktop.

 To initiate hibernation, activate the **Control Panel** and double-click the **Power Options** icon shown here. Then, in the displayed Power Options Properties dialogue box, click the Hibernate tab. If the Hibernate tab is unavailable, then this is because your computer does not support this feature. If it does, make sure the **Enable hibernation** box is checked, as shown in Fig. 9.21 on the next page.

Next, click the Advance tab and select what you want under **Options**, then click the down-arrow button against the **When I press the power button on my computer** box and choose what you want to happen from the drop-down options list shown in Fig. 9.22 also shown on the next page.

Fig. 9.21 The Power Options Properties Screen.

Fig. 9.22 The Power Button Options List.

Finally, click the Power Schemes tab, and select a time in **System hibernates**, as shown in Fig. 9.23. If you set this to, say, 'after 1 min', then you can sit back and see what happens. With our system, after one minute we were informed that it was safe to switch off the computer, which we did. When switching on the computer a few seconds later, Windows XP started up automatically and loaded all the programs that happened to be loaded at the time of hibernation.

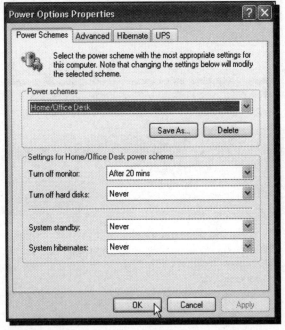

Fig. 9.23 The Power Options Power Scheme

Obviously this is a time saver much favoured by users of laptop computers. However, there is no reason why users of desktop computers should not also be in favour of this power saving management.

If you decide that you do not want your system to hibernate, just go through the procedure described above and uncheck the selected option in the Power Options Properties screen of Fig. 9.21. Finally, click the Power Schemes tab, and select 'never' for the time the **System hibernates**.

Standby Mode

When your computer is put into standby mode, information in computer memory is not saved to your hard disc. You must save all your work before putting your computer into standby mode, because if there is an interruption in power, all information in the computer's memory will be lost.

To initiate standby mode, activate the Control Panel and click on the Power Options icon. In the displayed Power Options Properties dialogue box, click the Power Schemes tab, as shown in Fig. 9.23.

If you are using a portable computer, you can specify one setting for battery power and a different setting for AC power. In fact, you can adjust any power management option that your computer's hardware configuration supports.

On Turning your Computer Off

As we have seen at the beginning of this book, you turn off your computer by the sequence *start*, **Turn Off Computer**, which displays a screen similar to the one in Fig. 9.24 below.

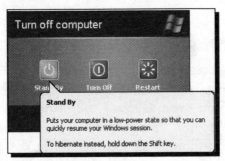

Fig. 9.24 The Turn Off Computer Box.

This exact box is displayed only if you have logged on as an administrator, your computer is set up by the manufacturer to support the two power management options of Standby and Hibernate, and you have to make sure that the **Enable hibernation** box is checked in Fig. 9.21.

Provided all of the above conditions are satisfied, then you can put your computer into immediate standby by clicking the **Stand By** button, or into hibernation by holding the <shift> key down, which causes the **Stand By** button to change to **Hibernate**, and clicking it. This has the effect of putting your computer into either of these two modes for this time only, unlike the procedures described earlier which are effective each time you switch off. Personally, we prefer this method of power management, as it is dependent on what you intend to do next, and it suits varying circumstances.

Backing up your Data

Hard discs can 'crash' (though not as often these days as they used to) or your PC could be stolen, or lost in a fire or flood. Any of these events would cause a serious data loss, unless you had backed up all your data on a regular basis, and stored it somewhere safely, preferably away from the vicinity of your PC.

Although Microsoft includes with Windows XP Professional Edition a **Backup** program, we will not discuss it here but will suggest an alternative procedure. After all, users of Windows XP Home Edition have just as important data that needs to be backed up!

Making a Back-up

Before we start making a back-up, it will be convenient to have the destination of the back-up on the **SendTo** folder. Although we have discussed this, as well as all the other procedures required in making a back-up in Chapter 3, we will put these together here, as we feel the subject is extremely important. You should get into the habit of making a back-up at least once a week.

The destination for the back-up could be an external hard disc, a zip drive, or a CD recorder. In the latter case, you will need a recordable compact disc (CD-R) or a rewritable compact disc (CD-RW). Since these days most users have a computer with a CD rewriter, we will use this as the back-up destination in our example, although you can apply the procedure to any of the other media mentioned above, even to floppy discs, if you have an endless supply of them.

To add a new location to the **Send To** menu, do the following:

- Click *start*, **My Computer**, and select the **Documents and Settings** folder on the drive where Windows XP is installed.

- Double-click the folder of a specific user.

- If the **SendTo** folder is not visible, use the **Tools, Folder Options** command, click the View tab, click the **Show hidden files and folders** option, and click the **Apply** button. Double-click the now visible **SendTo** folder.

- Use the **File, New, Shortcut** command, as shown in Fig. 9.25, and follow the instructions on your screen specifying your chosen backup drive.

Fig. 9.25 Adding a Shortcut to the SendTo Folder.

To start the back-up process, insert a blank recordable or rewritable CD in the CD recorder (or whatever other media you have chosen for your back-up into an appropriate drive), then do the following:

- Use **My Computer** to locate and select the files or folders you want to back up, as shown in Fig. 9.26 below.

Fig. 9.26 Selecting Folder to Back Up.

- While selecting your files or folder, keep the <Ctrl> key depressed if the files or folders you want to back up are not contiguous on the displayed list. In our example above, we chose to back up the highlighted folders on our D: drive.

- Next, and while these files or folders are selected and the <Ctrl> key <u>is still depressed,</u> right-click near your selection, and on the displayed menu choose the **Properties** option. We do this in order to find out the size of the selected items, as shown in Fig. 9.27 below.

Fig. 9.27 The Size of Selected Items.

As you can see, the selected folders require 1.30 GB of disc space and, naturally, will not fit on a 650 MB CD. However, in this case, the size of the Books folder, which contains compressed folders, is 846 MB, therefore we will need one CD to copy the books folder, and another for the rest of the selection. Whether you compress these folders or not, before making the back-up, is a matter of choice. If you do decide to compress them, do so one at a time.

To continue with the back-up process, do the following:

- Select the folders that will fit on one CD (or your chosen back-up media).

- While still holding the <Ctrl> key depressed, right-click near your selection and choose the **Send To** option, then click the back-up destination drive - drive J: in our case, as shown in Fig. 9.28.

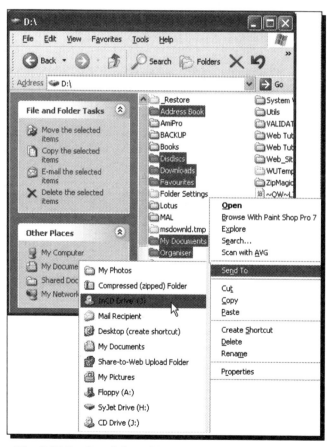

Fig. 9.28 Sending Selected Items to Back-up Media.

- After the selected folders have been transferred to our chosen back-up drive (in our example this being a CD writer), they are first prepared before starting to burn the CD, as shown in Fig. 9.29.

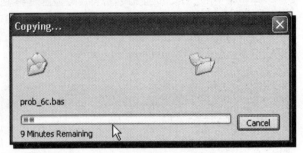

Fig. 9.29 Copying Files and Folders.

- Once all Files and Folders are copied into memory, they are ready to be written to CD, as shown in Fig. 9.30.

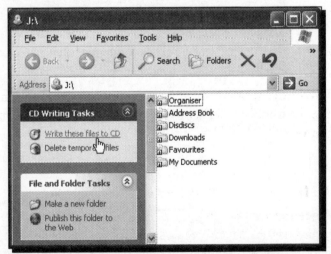

Fig. 9.30 Files and Folders Ready for Writing to CD.

- Next, click the **Write these files to CD** Tasks option which starts the CD Writing Wizard, shown in Fig. 9.31 below.

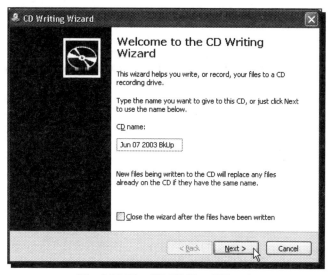

Fig. 9.31 The CD Writing Wizard.

- Give the back-up media a suitable name with the date of the back-up, then click **Next** to burn the selected files and folders onto a CD.

Obviously if you have selected a different back-up media, the instructions for copying will be different from the above.

Retrieving Back-up Files

Once the writing process is finished, transfer the CD into your CD-ROM drive and examine its contents. You should find a complete duplicate of all the selected files and folders, as shown in Fig. 9.32 on the next page.

Fig. 9.32 The Back-up List of Items.

To restore data from your back-up media, simply copy it back to the place it first came from. In our example this will be the D: drive.

Adding Files and Folders to a Back-up

To add files and folders to a back-up, even with a CD-R as is the case in our example, select the required files or folder and send it to the back-up drive. This will only succeed provided the addition of these files or folder to the existing back-up does not cause it to exceed the capacity of the media.

In Fig. 9.33 on the next page, we show the contents of our back-up CD, after adding to it a folder from our D: drive.

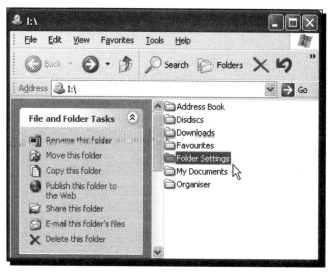

Fig. 9.33 The New Back-up List of Items.

We hope we have convinced you how easy it is and how necessary to make regular back-ups of your important data. Believe us, there is nothing more devastating than losing all your letters, pictures, videos, and all the other items you treasure so much for the sake of spending half an hour or so every week. Good luck!

10

Glossary of Terms

Access control	A security mechanism that determines which operations a user is authorised to perform on a PC, a file, a printer, etc.
Active	Describes the folder, window or icon that you are currently using or that is currently selected.
Active partition	A partition from which an x86-based computer starts up. The active partition must be a primary partition on a basic disc.
Address	A unique number or name that identifies a specific computer or user on a network.
Administrator	For Windows XP Professional, a person responsible for setting up and managing local computers, their user and group accounts, and assigning passwords and permissions.
Application	Software (program) designed to carry out a certain activity, such as word processing, or data management.

Association	An identification of a filename extension to a program. This lets Windows open the program when its files are selected.
AVI	Audio Video Interleaved. A Windows multimedia file format for sound and moving pictures.
Background	The screen background image used on a graphical user interface such as Windows.
Backup	To make a back-up copy of a file or a disc for safekeeping.
Bandwidth	The range of transmission frequencies a network can use. The greater the bandwidth the more information that can be transferred over a network.
Banner	An advertising graphic shown on a Web page.
Baud rate	The speed at which a modem communicates.
BBS	Bulletin Board System, a computer equipped with software and telecoms links that acts as an information host for remote computer systems.
Bit	The smallest unit of information handled by a computer.

Bitmap	A technique for managing the image displayed on a computer screen.
Bookmark	A marker inserted at a specific point in a document to which the user may wish to return for later reference.
Broadband	A communications system in which the medium of transmission (such as a wire or fibre-optic cable) carries multiple messages at a time.
Broadcast	An address that is destined for all hosts on a particular network segment.
Browse	A button in some Windows dialogue boxes that lets you view a list of files and folders before you make a selection.
Browser	A program, like the Internet Explorer, that lets you view Web pages.
Bug	An error in coding or logic that causes a program to malfunction.
Button	A graphic element in a dialogue box or toolbar that performs a specified function.
Bytes	A unit of data that holds a single character, such as a letter, a digit.

Cable modem	A device that enables a broadband connection to the Internet by using cable television infrastructure.
Cache	An area of memory, or disc space, reserved for data, which speeds up downloading.
CD-R	Recordable compact disc.
CD-ROM	Read Only Memory compact disc. Data can be read but not written.
CD-RW	Rewritable compact disc. Data can be copied to the CD on more than one occasion and can be erased.
Click	To press and release a mouse button once without moving the mouse.
Client	A computer that has access to services over a computer network. The computer providing the services is a server.
Clipboard	A temporary storage area of memory, where text and graphics are stored with the Windows cut and copy actions.
Command	An instruction given to a computer to carry out a particular action.
Compressed file	One that is compacted to save server space and reduce transfer times. A typical file extension for compressed files is .zip for Windows.

Configuration	A general purpose term referring to the way you have your computer set up.
Cookies	Files stored on your hard drive by your Web browser that hold information for it to use.
CPU	The Central Processing Unit; the main chip that executes all instructions entered into a computer.
Cyberspace	Originated by William Gibson in his novel 'Neuromancer', now used to describe the Internet and the other computer networks.
Default	The command, device or option automatically chosen.
Defragmentation	The process of rewriting parts of a file to contiguous sectors on a hard disc to increase the speed of access and retrieval.
Desktop	The Windows screen working background, on which you place icons, folders, etc.
Device driver	A special file that must be loaded into memory for Windows to be able to address a specific procedure or hardware device.
Device name	A logical name used to identify a device, such as LPT1 or COM1 for the parallel or serial printer.

Dial-up connection	The connection to a network via a device that uses the telephone network. This includes modems with a standard phone line, ISDN cards with high-speed ISDN lines.
Dialogue box	A window displayed on the screen to allow the user to enter information.
Digital signature	A means for originators of a message, file, or other digitally encoded information to bind their identity to the information.
Directory	An area on disc where information relating to a group of files is kept. Also known as a folder.
Disconnect	To detach a drive, port or computer from a shared device, or to break an Internet connection.
DLL	Dynamic Link Library; An OS feature that allows files with the .dll extensions to be loaded only when needed by the program.
Document	A file produced by an application program. When used in reference to the Web, a document is any file containing text, media or hyperlinks that can be transferred from an HTTP server to a browser.
Domain	A group of devices, servers and computers on a network.

Domain Name	The name of an Internet site, for example www.microsoft.com, which allows you to reference Internet sites without knowing their true numerical address.
Double-click	To quickly press and release a mouse button twice.
Download	To transfer to your computer a file, or data, from another computer.
DPI	Dots Per Inch - a resolution standard for laser printers.
Drag	To move an object on the screen by pressing and holding down the left mouse button while moving the mouse.
Drive name	The letter followed by a colon which identifies a floppy or hard disc drive.
DSL	Digital Subscriber Line - a broad-band connection to the Internet through existing copper telephone wires.
DVD	Digital Video Disc; a type of optical disc technology. It looks like a CD but can store greater amounts of data.
E-mail	Electronic Mail - A system that allows computer users to send and receive messages electronically.

Encrypted password	A password that is scrambled.
Engine	Software used by search services.
Extract a file	Create an uncompressed copy of the file in a folder you specify.
FAQ	Frequently Asked Questions - A common feature on the Internet, FAQs are files of answers to commonly asked questions.
FAT	The File Allocation Table. An area on disc where information is kept on which part of the disc a file is located.
File extension	The suffix following the period in a filename. Windows uses this to identify the source application program. For example .jpg indicates a graphic file.
Filename	The name given to a file. In Windows this can be up to 256 characters long.
Filter	A set of criteria that is applied to data to show a subset of the data.
Firewall	Security measures designed to protect a networked system, or a PC, from unauthorised access.
Floppy disc	A removable disc on which information can be stored magnetically.

Folder	An area used to store a group of files, usually with a common link.
Font	A graphic design representing a set of characters, numbers and symbols.
Format	The structure of a file that defines the way it is stored and laid out on the screen or in print.
Fragmentation	The scattering of parts of the same file over different areas of the disc.
Function key	One of the series of 10 or 12 keys marked with the letter F and a numeral, used for specific operations.
GIF	Graphics Interchange Format, a common standard for images on the Web.
Gigabyte	(GB); 1,024 megabytes. Usually thought of as one billion bytes.
Graphic	A picture or illustration, also called an image. Formats include GIF, JPEG, BMP, PCX, and TIFF.
Group	A collection of users, computers, contacts, and other groups.
Handshaking	A series of signals acknowledging that communication can take place between computers or other devices.
Hard copy	Output on paper.

Hard disc	A device built into the computer for holding programs and data.
Hardware	The equipment that makes up a computer system, excluding the programs or software.
Help	A Windows system that gives you instructions and additional information on using a program.
Hibernation	A state in which your computer shuts down after saving everything in memory on your hard disc.
Home page	The document displayed when you first open your Web browser, or the first document you come to at a Web site.
Host	Computer connected directly to the Internet that provides services to other local and/or remote computers.
HTML	HyperText Markup Language, the format used in documents on the Web.
Hyperlink	A segment of text, or an image, that refers to another document on the Web, an intranet or your PC.
Hypertext	A system that allows documents to be cross-linked so that the reader can explore related links, or documents, by clicking on a highlighted symbol.

Icon	A small graphic image that represents a function or object. Clicking on an icon produces an action.
Image	See graphic.
Insertion point	A flashing bar that shows where typed text will be entered into a document.
Interface	A device that allows you to connect a computer to its peripherals.
Internet	The global system of computer networks.
Intranet	A private network inside an organisation using the same kind of software as the Internet.
IP	Internet Protocol - The rules that provide basic Internet functions.
IP Address	Internet Protocol Address - every computer on the Internet has a unique identifying number.
ISDN	Integrated Services Digital Network; a telecom standard using digital transmission technology to support voice, video and data communications applications over regular telephone lines.

ISP	Internet Service Provider - A company that offers access to the Internet.
JPEG / JPG	Joint Photographic Experts Group, a popular cross-platform format for image files. JPEG is best suited for true colour original images.
Kilobyte	(KB); 1024 bytes of information or storage space.
LAN	Local Area Network - High-speed, privately-owned network covering a limited geographical area, such as an office or a building.
Laptop	A portable computer small enough to sit on your lap.
Links	The hypertext connections between Web pages.
Local	A resource that is located on your computer, not linked to it over a network.
Location	An Internet address.
Log on	To gain access to a network, or the Internet.
Megabyte	(MB); 1024 kilobytes of information or storage space.
Megahertz	(MHz); Speed of processor in millions of cycles per second.

Memory	Part of computer consisting of storage elements organised into addressable locations that can hold data and instructions.
Menu	A list of available options in an application.
Menu bar	The horizontal bar that lists the names of menus.
Modem	Short for Modulator-demodulator. An electronic device that lets computers communicate electronically.
Monitor	The display device connected to your PC, also called a screen.
Mouse	A device used to manipulate a pointer around your display and activate processes by pressing buttons.
MPEG	Motion Picture Experts Group - a video file format offering excellent quality in a relatively small file.
Multimedia	The use of photographs, music and sound and movie images in a presentation.
Multitasking	Performing more than one operation at the same time.
My Documents	A folder that provides a convenient place to store documents, graphics,

	or other files you want to access quickly.
Network	Two or more computers connected together to share resources.
Network server	Central computer which stores files for several linked computers.
NTFS file system	An advanced file system that provides performance, security, reliability, and advanced features that are not found in any version of FAT.
Online	Having access to the Internet.
On-line Service	Services such as America On-line and CompuServe that provide content to subscribers and usually connections to the Internet.
Operating system	Software that runs a computer.
Page	An HTML document, or Web site.
Parallel port	The input/output connector for a parallel interface device. Printers are normally plugged into a parallel port.
Partition	A portion of a physical disc that functions as though it were a physically separate disc.
Password	A unique character string used to gain access to a network, program, or mailbox.

Peripheral	Any device attached to a PC.
Pixel	The smallest picture element on screen that can be independently assigned colour and intensity.
Plug-and-play	Hardware which can be plugged into a PC and be used immediately without configuration.
POP	Post Office Protocol - a method of storing and returning e-mail.
Port	The place where information goes into or out of a computer, such as a modem.
Portal	A Web site that is the first place people see when using the Web. Typically a 'Portal site' has a catalogue of web sites, a search engine, or both, and it may also offer e-mail and other services.
PostScript	A page-description language (PDL), developed by Adobe Systems for printing on laser printers.
Print queue	A list of print jobs waiting to be sent to a printer.
Program	A set of instructions which cause a computer to perform tasks.
Protocol	A set of rules or standards that define how computers communicate with each other.

Queue	A list of e-mail messages waiting to be sent over the Internet, or files to a printer.
RAM	Random Access Memory. The computer's volatile memory. Data held in it is lost when power is switched off.
Refresh	To update displayed information with current data.
Registered file type	File types that are tracked by the system registry and are recognised by the programs you have installed on your computer.
Registry	A database where information about a PC's configuration is deposited. The registry contains information that Windows continually references during its operation.
Remote computer	A computer that you can access only by using a communications line or a communications device, such as a network card or a modem.
ROM	Read Only Memory. A PC's non-volatile memory. Data is written into this memory at manufacture and is not affected by power loss.
Screen saver	A moving picture, pattern, or series of pictures, that appears on your screen when you have not used the

	mouse or keyboard for a specified period of time.
Scroll bar	A bar that appears at the right side or bottom edge of a window.
Search	Submit a query to a search engine.
Search engine	A program that helps users find information across the Internet.
Serial interface	An interface that transfers data as individual bits.
Server	A computer system that manages and delivers information for client computers.
Shared resource	Any device, program or file that is available to network users.
Shortcut	A link to any item accessible on your computer or on a network, such as a program, file, folder, disc drive, Web page, printer, or another computer.
Signature file	A text file, maintained within e-mail programs, that contains text for your signature.
Site	A place on the Internet. Every Web page has a location where it resides which is called its site.
Software	The programs and instructions that control your PC.

Spooler	Software which handles the transfer of information to a store to be used by a peripheral device.
Standby	A state in which your computer consumes less power when it is idle, but remains available for immediate use.
Subscribe	To become a member of.
Surfing	The process of looking around the Internet.
Swap file	An area of your hard disc used to store temporary operating files, also known as virtual memory.
System disc	A disc containing files to enable a PC to start up.
System files	Files used by Windows to load, configure, and run the operating system.
Task Manager	A utility that provides information about programs and processes running on the computer. Using Task Manager, you can end or run programs and end processes, and display a dynamic overview of your computer's performance.
TCP/IP	Transmission Control Protocol/ Internet Protocol, combined protocols that perform the transfer of data between two computers. TCP

	monitors and ensures the correct transfer of data. IP receives the data, breaks it up into packets, and sends it to a network within the Internet.
Text file	An unformatted file of text characters.
TIFF	Tag Image File Format - a popular graphic image file format.
Toggle	To turn an action on and off with the same switch.
Tool	Software program used to support Web site creation and management.
Toolbar	A bar containing icons giving quick access to commands.
Uninstall	When referring to software, the act of removing program files and folders from your hard disc and removing related data from your registry so the software is no longer available.
Upload/Download	The process of transferring files between computers. Files are uploaded from your computer to another and downloaded from another computer to your own.
URL	Uniform Resource Locator, the addressing system used on the Web, containing information about the method of access, the server to be

	accessed and the path of the file to be accessed.
USB	Universal Serial Bus - an external bus standard that enables data transfer rates of 12 Mbps.
User ID	The unique identifier, usually used in conjunction with a password, which identifies you on a computer.
Virus	A malicious program, downloaded from a web site or disc, designed to wipe out information on your computer.
WAV	Waveform Audio (.wav) - a common audio file format.
Web	A network of hypertext-based multimedia information servers. Browsers are used to view any information on the Web.
Web Page	An HTML document that is accessible on the Web.
Web server	A computer that is maintained by a system administrator or Internet service provider (ISP) and that responds to requests from a user's browser.
Wizard	A Microsoft tool that asks you questions and then creates an object depending on your answers.

Index

A

Accessibility options. 153
Accessories. 4, 53, 79, 172
Active window. . . . 11, 34
Adding
   new hardware. 83
   software. 84
   to Favorites. 142
   to Start menu. 6
   Windows features. . . 85
Address
   Bar. 10, 13
   Bar (Internet Expl). 137
   Book. 80, 127
Application windows. . 21
Arrange
   desktop icons. 9
   windows. 38
Attachments (e-mail). 111
Automatic Update. . . 180

B

Back-up data files. . . . 201
Bitmap files. 168
Block senders list. . . . 126
Burning CDs. . 57, 72, 180

C

Cascade
   menus. 3, 53
   windows. 38
Category view . . . 66, 166
Changing
   active window. 34
   default printer. 73
   display settings. 68
   Taskbar menus. 33
Check boxes. 28
Classic view. 66, 166
Cleanup discs. 188
Clipboard. 48
Clock. 34, 87
Close
   button. 10, 13
   window. 36
Command button. . 10, 12
Common
   Toolbar buttons. 23
Communications . . . 3, 79
Compressing folders. . . 61
Configuring printers. . . 73
Contacts pane. 99
Control Panel views. . . 65
Copy
   command. 48
   files/folders. 48, 60

Create
    Dial-up connection. . 96
    Internet connection. . 91
    new folder. 42
    new message. 97
    shortcut. 53
    System restore point 186
Customise a Toolbar. . . 23

D

Date/Time settings. 34, 87
Default
    printer. 73
    Web site. 134
Defragmenting discs. . 191
Delete files/folder. 54
Desktop. 32
    customise. 53, 57
    icons. 9
    shortcut menu. 9
Dialogue boxes. 27
Disc
    cleanup. 188
    defragmenting. . . . 191
    error scanning. . . . 189
Display
    accessibility. 156
    properties. 68
Download updates. . . 183
Drag and Drop. 49

E

E-mail. 89
    attachments. 111
Edit menu command. . . 26
Electronic mail. 89
Empty Recycle Bin. . . 55
Exit Windows 19
Explorer bar. 26

F

Favorites. 140
    menu command. 26
Fax
    Console. 79
    printer. 75
    Utility. 80
File
    compression. 61
    copying. 48, 60
    deleting. 54
    find. 44
    menu command. 26
    moving. 48
    properties. 63
    renaming. 43
    search. 44
    selecting. 47
    sending. 50
    system. 45
Filename
    convention. 45
    extensions. 29, 45

Filmstrip view. 59
Finding
   files/folders. 44
Firewall. 187
Folder
   compression. 61
   copying. 48, 60
   create new. 42
   deleting. 54
   finding. 44
   list (Outlook). 98
   moving. 48
   Options. 27, 50
   Printers & Faxes. . . . 71
   Properties. 203
   renaming. 43
   search. 44
   selecting. 47
   sending. 50
Folders list (Outlook). . 98
Fonts. 67, 72, 156

G
Graphics files. . . . 45, 112

H
Hardware
   adding. 83
Help
   Address Book. 82
   file. 45
   Internet Explorer. . . 150
   menu command. 27

Outlook Express. . . 130
   system. 17
Hibernation mode. . . . 196
History facility. 143
Home Toolbar button. 145
Hotmail. 146

I
Icons arrangement. . . . 9
Icon shortcuts. 53
Image
   folder views. 57
   previewing. 58
Insert attachment. . . . 111
Installing
   fax printer. 75
   printers. 71
Internet
   Address Bar. 137
   Connection Wizard. . 91
   Explorer. 131
   Favorites. 140
   Help. 150
   History files. 143
   Hotmail. 146
   Searching. 134
   Service Provider 93, 132
   Standard Toolbar. . 138

K
Keyboard
   accessibility. 155
   on-screen. 163

L

Language settings. 86
List in dialogue box. . . 28

M

Magnifier. 161
Manipulating windows. 34
Maximise
  button. 10, 12
  window. 36
Menu
  bar. 10, 25, 13
  cascade. 3, 53
  options. 25
  Send to. 50
  shortcuts. 9
Message (Outlook)
  Blocked message list126
  formatting. 107
  list. 99
  Preview 100
  Preview pane 100
  printing. 122
  Rules. 123
  stationery. 106
  status icons. 101
  Toolbar. 102
Minimise
  button. 10, 12
  window. 36
Modem properties. . . . 89

Mouse

Accessibility. 157
pointer(s). 10, 16, 13, 16
right-clicking. 9
Movie Maker. 172
Moving
  dialogue boxes. 35
  files/folders. 48
  windows. 35
My Computer. . . . 10, 21

N

New
  Connection Wizard. 131
  contact. 81
  folder. 42
  Hardware Wizard. . . 83
  message (Outlook). 105

O

Open an attachment. . 115
Option buttons. 29
Organise messages. . . 115
Outlook Express. 90
  Help. 130
  window. 98

P

Paste command. 48
Picture & Fax viewer. . 58
Pixels. 68
Plug & Play. 72, 83
Pointers. 16

Power management. . 196
Preview
   image. 58
   pane (Outlook). . . . 100
Print queue. 74
Printer
   configuration. 73
   installation. 72
   properties. 73
Printers & Faxes folder. 71
Printing
   messages (Outlook). 122
Problem prevention. . 179
Program associations. . 45
Properties window. 22, 33

Q
Quick launch icons. . . . 32

R
Radio buttons. 29
Read message
   Toolbar. 104
   window. 103
Receiving attachments 114
Recycle Bin. 55
   shortcut menu. 9
Regional settings. 86
Remove
   Outlook messages. . 109
   programs. 84
   Start menu entries. . . . 6
   Windows features. . . 85

Rename
   file/folder. 43
   Start menu entries. . . . 8
Replying to messages. 109
Resize windows. 36
Restart Windows. 20
Restoring
   system. 184
   window size. . . . 12, 36
Right-click menus. 9

S
Save attachment. 115
Scanning
   discs. 189
   pictures. 166
Scheduled tasks. 192
Screen
   resolution. 68
   savers. 69
   themes. 69
Scroll bar(s). 10, 13
Search
   facility. 18, 44, 151
   files/folders. 44
   Internet. 134
Selecting
   e-mail recipients. . . 128
   files/folders. 47
Send To command. . . . 50
Sending
   a Fax. 76
   e-mail attachments. 111

files/folders 50
scanned pictures. . . 171
video clips. 172
Settings Regional. 86
Setup. 90, 132
Shortcut
creation. 53
icons. 9
menus. 9
Show hidden files. . . . 202
Shutdown option. 19, 196
Signing an e-mail. . . . 104
Sizing windows. 35
Software adding. 115
Sound Accessibility. . 155
Spell checking. 118
Standard Toolbar. . . . 138
Standby mode. 198
Start
button. 2, 5, 10, 17
menu. 2, 33
Status bar. . . 26, 133, 138
System
file protection. 180
folders (Outlook). . 116
information. 179
restore. 184
tools. 179, 184
updates. 180

T
Tab key. 27
Tabbed dialogue box. . 27
Task bar. 10, 32
buttons. 32
menus. 33
Tasks
menus. 43
pane. 10, 14
scheduling. 192
Tile windows. 38, 39
Time setting. 34, 87
Title bar. . . 10, 12, 23, 35
Toolbar. 10, 13, 23
Tools menu command. 27
Turn off computer 19, 200

U
Undo command. 24
Update Windows. . . . 180
URL address. 137
User accounts. 5
Using Help System. . . . 17

V
View
command. 15
Explorer bar. 26
menu command. . . . 26
Toolbars. 23, 25

W

Wav files. 45
Web
    search. 134
    site. 134, 180
What's This?. 23
Window
    arranging. 38
    closing. 36
    command button. 10, 12
    maximising. 36
    minimising. 36
    moving. 35
    resizing. 35
Windows
    applications. 3, 16
    automatic update. . . 180
    Control Panel. 65
    desktop. 2, 9, 14
    environment. 21
    folder. 50
    Help system. 17
    screen. 2, 10
Wizards
    Add New Hardware. 83
    Add Printer. 71
    Scheduled tasks. . . . 192

Z

Zipped folders. 61

Companion Discs

COMPANION DISCS are available for most computer books written by the same author(s) and published by BERNARD BABANI (publishing) LTD, as listed at the front of this book (except for those marked with an asterisk). These books contain many pages of file/program listings.

There is no Companion Disc for this book.

To obtain companion discs for other books, fill in the order form below, or a copy of it, enclose a cheque (payable to **P.R.M. Oliver**) or a postal order, and send it to the address given below. **Make sure you fill in your name and address** and specify the book number and title in your order.

Book No.	Book Name	Unit Price	Total Price
BP		£3.50	
BP		£3.50	
BP		£3.50	
Name .... Address		Sub-total	£.............
		P & P (@ 45p/disc)	£.............
		Total Due	£.............
Send to: P.R.M. Oliver, West Trevarth House, West Trevarth, Nr Redruth, Cornwall, TR16 5TJ			

PLEASE NOTE

The author(s) are fully responsible for providing this Companion Disc service. The publishers of this book accept no responsibility for the supply, quality, or magnetic contents of the disc, or in respect of any damage, or injury that might be suffered or caused by its use.